"Mom, I Got a Tattoo*!"
*The Survival Guide to Raising a
Teenage Daughter

DR. JANET IRWIN, SUSANNA DE VRIES

Robins Lane Press
a division of Gryphon House, Inc.

www.robinslane.com

Library of Congress Cataloging-in-Publication Data

Irwin, Janet.
    Mom, I got a tattoo!: the survival guide to raising a teenage
daughter / Janet Irwin and Susanna de Vries.
        p.   cm.
    ISBN 1-58904-011-2
    1. Teenage girls—Family relationships. 2. Teenage girls—
Counseling of. 3. Parent and teenager.   I. De Vries, Susanna.
II. Title.
HQ798.I783   2001
649'.133—dc21   2001044100

IMPORTANT NOTE: All care is taken to ensure that information contained in this book is free from error and/or omissions; however no responsibility can be accepted by the publisher, contributors, distributors or editor for loss and/or damage to any person acting or refraining from action as a result of material contained in this book. Before commencing any health treatment, always consult your doctor.

Published by Robins Lane Press
A division of Gryphon House
10726 Tucker St., Beltsville, MD 20704 U.S.A.
Copyright © 2001 by Dr. Janet Irwin and Susanna de Vries
International Standard Book Number: 1-58904-011-2

CONTENTS

A TIME OF TRANSITION

What Has Happened to Your Daughter?

The little bundle in your arms with wispy hair and tiny, perfect fingers drew an overwhelming surge of tenderness and protectiveness from you. How and when did that sweet baby turn into this angry adolescent girl whose behavior makes you grind your teeth with frustration and despair?

You and Your Adolescent Daughter

Your daughter will be well on her way to adolescence by the age of twelve. She knows a great deal about you, but you will be living with a chameleon. Just as you have adjusted to one development and think you have her figured out, she will change again.

Remember your own adolescence—unfamiliar body, unpredictable moods and undefined yearnings? Remember the fights with your parents when they treated you as a child but demanded you behave like an adult? The rites of passage were often as exhilarating and stomach churning as a roller-coaster ride.

Now your daughter faces exactly the same confusion and struggle for self-knowledge that you did. The transition from child to adult is a tough one, particularly if you, as a loving and concerned parent, are determined to control the process and the outcome.

You can help her or make it harder. Your role as parent is to teach your daughter life skills that will guide her through the minefields ahead. Even though she is on the threshold of adulthood and your relationship is changing, *you* remain her parent. She looks to you for security, consistency and guidance. It is not your role to be a competitive parent or to be her pal. She will find pals among her own age group.

Adolescence is often a war of independence. You can win battles, but finally she must win the war.

Are You Ready to Loosen the Reins?

As she grows older, your daughter will spend more and more time away from home and be exposed to temptations and dangers that give you nightmares. She will start high school, travel alone and want to go out at night to a dance or to the movies with a boy. With your permission, she will stay overnight at girlfriends' homes.

You will be filled with anxiety and believe that things will go dreadfully wrong, unless you keep a close eye on everything your daughter does. This means you can't come to terms with your diminished role in her life. But in many things you *have* to trust her, even more so as she gets older. If you want to build a mature relationship with her, be prepared to forgive mistakes and hope she learns from them. Don't hold on too tight to the reins—if you do, sooner or later you may lose control and the horse will bolt.

TIPS FOR PARENTING AN ADOLESCENT DAUGHTER

- Spend exclusive time with your daughter, giving her your undivided attention. Chat while doing dishes together. Go out together for coffee or a soda. You don't always have to spend money. Try going for a walk. It's important to set aside some time when you can relax together.

- Share jokes, exchange gossip, relate family anecdotes and laugh at mistakes. Be positive with her so that she sees you as a relaxed, communicative person—not just a tense, serious parent.

- Have family meals together without the TV blaring. Involve everyone in helping to set the table, pick flowers and serve food. Don't use mealtime to settle scores—it spoils the occasion. Teach your daughter to cook *her* favorite dishes, and allow her to ask friends for dinner. Adolescent friends love being invited to impromptu meals, and on such informal occasions "hard" topics such as drugs, alcoholism and contraception may crop up spontaneously in discussion.

- Remember that children copy their parents and adults they admire. Good manners, confidence, poise and consideration for others are developed at home.

- Don't criticize your daughter continually. If your exchanges are limited to her shortcomings, you are reacting only to misbehavior.

- Compliment your daughter for a job well done, for persevering with an unpleasant task, for showing self-control, for taking the trouble to look great. Draw attention to accomplishments: success at school, at work or in sports. Praise her for good behavior and performance. Acknowledge thoughtfulness; don't take it for granted.

- Treat your daughter with respect. Adolescents are reasonable beings . . . sometimes! Adults can be difficult too. Let her know if you are under pressure, and ask for her understanding. Extend the same to her in return. You can't always be the perfect parent, and she shouldn't expect it. Teach by example. She will appreciate the courtesy of an apology.

- Mothers know how fragile and tired they may get before their periods, so they can sympathize with their daughter's premenstrual tension, stomach cramps and headaches. Remind other family members to "go easy" at this time.

- Pressure from school commitments may also put your daughter under stress. Projects, homework, extracurricular activities and parental expectations put conscientious students under enormous pressure. Does your daughter need to reassess her commitments? Help her to do so.

- Death or illness of a family member, of a friend or of household pets can be devastating. Loss of employment, parental conflict or a move to a new home can also cause serious stress in families. Adolescents react badly, often unaware of the reasons for their actions. If this has happened, make allowances.

■ Don't overburden your daughter with household chores. Is she expected to do more than a boy does just because she is a girl?

■ Encourage your daughter to think for herself and take responsibility for her own actions. You cannot make decisions for her forever. With a little guidance from you, allow her to make decisions when she is still young—it will build up her self-esteem and self-confidence, and she will learn from her mistakes.

■ Academic and career choices can be confusing. Get advice from the school counselor and go to job fairs. Assess your daughter's interests, strengths and weaknesses. Be flexible. Encourage her to keep her options open because her interests may change. She may want to be a pop singer at thirteen, but by sixteen she will have moved on. Changing direction is not the end of the world. Don't try to decide *her* future for her.

■ Comfort and reassure her when she is hurt, upset or disappointed. Ignoring her pain to "toughen her up" teaches her that the world is callous and unresponsive to her needs. Allowing her to confide in you when she has a problem will give you the opportunity to help her face the situation and put it in perspective.

■ Teenagers live in a vastly different world—technologically and economically—from the one in which you grew up. Of course, you cannot meet all her demands for the latest products. If you don't have the money, or if you have doubts about a proposed purchase, tell her. Advertising is aimed at adolescents to part them from their (and your) money. A set allowance or part-time job helps teenagers learn the value of money.

■ When your daughter, intent on forging her own identity, rejects your values, don't panic. She is testing what you have taught her against values she has encountered in the wider world. When she is most critical of you is often when she most needs you to be understanding—while at the same time angrily accusing you of "not understanding anything."

Finding Her Place in the World

Remember feeling oppressed and hemmed in, needing to burst out of the confines of home to get away and be by yourself? The world was beckoning. If you can remember this, you may understand your adolescent daughter much better.

Your daughter's physical and psychological growth leads to an intense curiosity about the world outside the family home. She is curious about how other people live and behave; she wants to experience alternative lifestyles and experiment with different looks. Boys are on her mind even if they haven't arrived on your doorstep.

Your adolescent daughter wants her own identity, and to have this she may feel that she must end her previous close association with you. It is very painful for parents to learn that their young daughter now keeps secrets from them. She resorts to hurtful stratagems to keep parents at arm's length. Friends seem far more important than parents. There are long telephone conversations, loud music behind closed bedroom doors and hours spent locked in the bathroom.

There may be dramatic changes in her appearance as she experiments with the "latest" look: gelled or multicolored hair, haircuts that make you shudder, makeup and nail polish suitable for pantomime characters and what you consider totally outrageous clothes. Teenage fads you loathe, she will find irresistible.

"Don't you trust me?" is the disingenuous reproach when you insist she be home by a reasonable hour or refuse her request to attend a party or sleepover at the house of people you don't know. And of course, you are the *only* parent with outdated ideas, such as calling to check whether there will be any adult supervision.

A major shift in the focus of your daughter's social and emotional life is occurring. This marks the beginning of a deliberate distancing from you—keeping you at a physical distance as well as emotionally separating from you. She wants to explore the world, discover where she fits into the scheme of things and establish her own identity. By now it becomes apparent that nature's fiendish sense of humor often deliberately mismatches parents and daughters. Quiet, retiring parents are saddled with boisterous girls; fashion-conscious parents are given "alternative" daughters with dreadlocks; out-of-doors no-frills parents get teenage fashion plates, eager to shop till they drop and acquire a gold credit card.

"Mom, I Got a Tattoo!"

The Survival Guide to Raising a
Teenage Daughter

CHAPTER 1

ROLE MODELS AND RELATIONSHIPS WITH FAMILY AND FRIENDS

Dangerous Role Models

The influence of 1960s feminists has irrevocably changed men's perception of women and women's perception of themselves. However, girls today find the portrayal of women in film and pop culture of the 1960s hilarious. Feminists' achievements are taken for granted in the postfeminist era. Most young women now refuse to call themselves feminists.

With whom do today's girls identify? Not with the feminists of the 1960s, nor with the superwomen of the past few decades like Geraldine Ferraro, Indira Gandhi and Madeline Albright who were then key players on an international stage. They have few equivalents today.

Whom does our popular press see as female role models or significant women? Britney Spears, Cameron Diaz and the next big supermodel are the stars of contemporary women's magazines and teen publications. The 1990s saw the emergence of supermodels as role models. For many girls they have become the epitome of the unattainable. Their physique—

height, slenderness and long legs—redefined the concept of feminine beauty. Should the superficial worlds of Hollywood and fashion modeling, where most actresses and models are commodities with a short shelf life, provide us with role models for impressionable girls? Why don't women's magazines run stories more often on courageous women, like those young female doctors who devote their lives to working in fistula or leprosy clinics and children's hospitals in the developing countries?

There are excellent role models in the professional world and in sports. Women's basketball and soccer leagues are gaining popularity and visibility. The women involved in these sports provide a strong and healthy image of female independence, ambition, and confidence. Unfortunately, today's newspapers, television programs, and magazines are still filled with stories about drug-addicted pop stars who attempt suicide with depressing frequency or lavish-spending younger female stars whose names are linked with many different men. Do women who are so obviously addicted to pleasure and narcissism make inspiring role models for young girls?

Lack of good role models or any belief system contributes to what some psychologists and teachers now define as "spiritual anorexia." This term means a depressive wasting away of the spirit and bleak nihilism. Girls from broken or abusive homes, who lack a positive belief system or family support, are at risk for spiritual anorexia. In some cases, such circumstances have caused depressive illness or even suicide. Other factors that may lead to spiritual anorexia include prolonged exposure to life-cheapening values such as the glorification of casual sex, gross materialism and a profound belief that it is impossible to save the world from pollution or destruction. We must see that girls receive positive messages and good role models to counteract this nihilistic approach to life. Strengthening relationships with family and trusted friends can help provide good role models.

Will the Mother-Daughter Bond Survive?

Mother-daughter relations veer from the close and companionable to the confrontational, competitive and tense—they swivel from one extreme to the other with head-spinning rapidity.

You have been the most important person in your daughter's formative years and will remain the most influential. Hence the advice to suitors: "Look at the mother to see what her daughter will become."

Little boys go through a stage of wanting to marry their mothers; little girls go through a stage of wanting to be them. They play with dolls and toys, dress up in their mothers' clothes and can be fascinated by the mystique of feminine garments, high heels, and perfume and by applying lipstick and eye makeup.

Many mothers find it difficult to come to terms with their adolescent daughters' struggle to find their own identities, particularly in cases when the mother was very close to her daughter during the early years. Boys start separating from their mothers around the age of six, when their interest shifts to their fathers or other male role models. A daughter's separation occurs during adolescence, when she focuses her emotional turmoil on her mother and expresses her rejection in searing criticism of many things her mother does. Girls' comments about their mothers' appearance, taste and personality can be exceedingly cruel.

It may help to remember that adolescent girls are *just* as hard on themselves. Women, old and young, put a lot of pressure on themselves and their daughters to be perfect. Males tend to be less self-critical.

Adolescent girls in particular are curious about others' lives—their friends, other mothers and other families. They make comparisons, and their own mothers are certainly not exempted from their cool analyses. Try not to be crushed by wounding remarks. It can help to compare notes (in private) with other mothers who are enduring the same criticisms. No matter how attractive or popular, teenage girls are uncertain of themselves and look for reassurance. Sometimes anything you say will be misinterpreted and you cannot do anything right. You may think she takes little notice of your opinion, but you know her better than any of her friends, and your comments will be taken to heart, although she may seem to ignore them.

Make time for her and be alert to her needs in what is, after all, a transitional stage in her development. As she gets older and more mature, you will find that the bond between you will strengthen again. She has every reason to trust you and will consult you when she has a family of her own. When you feel low, remember that daughters will be of comfort to you in your middle years and old age.

Is Dad Still Her Hero?

The relationship between father and daughter is different. There is that all-too-brief period when Dad is godlike and can do no wrong. He is the person on whom she practices charm and the gentle art of persuasion. Her first knowledge about men is acquired by spending time with him. She learns about trust and safety by doing things with him and learning from him.

When their daughters enter adolescence, dads sometimes become even more protective of their daughters than before, regarding other males as potential predators, heartbreakers and jerks who could use them. When a girl begins to be interested in boys, her father's feelings about this may be tinged with resentment and jealousy. But she needs his reassurance when her romance founders. It is Dad who must reassure her that she is irresistible in spite of her freckles and the braces on her teeth.

There are bleak periods when she regards her father as an ignorant, insensitive old stick-in-the-mud. Dad may never be her hero again, but, with any luck, she will eventually recognize his good intentions and devotion and be grateful for his loving care.

TIPS FOR FATHERS

■ Spend time with your young daughter *before* she reaches the turbulence of adolescence and draws away from you. Tell her stories, read to her, take her for walks, and go to the beach, the library or events you both enjoy.

■ Praise her strengths rather than criticize her weaknesses. Never regard her as second best because she is "only" a girl. Be as interested in her school results and career plans as in those of her brother(s). Make her feel you are convinced she can succeed in anything she wants to do. Teach her some traditionally "masculine" skills that will help her in the future, such as changing a fuse and pounding in a nail.

■ Try to attain a balance between the time you have to spend at work and your involvement with your daughter. It is your responsibility to show her that fathers are caring and affectionate beings. You are the role model for her future relationships with men.

■ Keep in mind that girls change from cute cuddly tots to prickly teenagers and become supercritical and moody. They become worried about their looks, their weight, their rapidly changing bodies and what everyone else thinks of them. It can be a hard time for fathers. At this time your daughter desperately needs your reassurance that she is still special to you and an attractive person. If her dentist advises she needs braces to straighten crooked teeth, think seriously about getting it done.

■ Before your daughter reaches puberty, tell her that she is far too special to be degraded by being used as a sexual convenience by a boy who is not interested in a mature relationship. Give her our chapter on "Sexually Transmitted Diseases" to read. In sex education or life preparation classes many girls simply stop paying attention, feeling such information does not apply to them. Point out it applies to everyone.

- Explain to your daughter that sex with a teenage boy is largely unromantic and disappointing—it is nothing like Hollywood movies, and it rarely leads to the type of romantic closeness she may dream about. Your daughter should understand that feelings of lust that teenagers experience have little to do with genuine love. Sex should be founded on a prolonged and meaningful relationship.
- Once you consider your daughter mature enough to borrow your car, make her sign a contract whereby she pays your deductible and all damage not covered by insurance if she crashes it. When she goes out, agree on a time when she will return, and if she doesn't return home at the agreed hour or phone you before that time, refuse to loan her the car for a stated period.

Role of Friends and Relatives

Your friends are an important source of support, companionship and social contact for you and your family. They are sometimes closer and more understanding than relatives are and, when relatives are far away, they can assume the roles of family. Close friends have the potential to be seen as role models by your children and can be called upon for assistance, if the need arises. They are not caught up in the emotional turmoil that often exists in families, but they are sufficiently close, loved and trusted to be consulted if necessary.

Being invited to stay with close family friends or relatives for a few days is often a welcome change for the adolescent, who feels she is away from all that parental scrutiny and nagging. The parents also benefit from having breathing space. The opportunity to discuss matters of interest with an adult other than a parent or teacher is usually welcomed by teenagers. It is amazing how much more "adult" daughters seem when they have been away from home for a week or two and experienced life in another household.

Through your daughter you will meet other parents, teachers and coaches at school, sporting and social functions. Get to know the parents of your daughter's friends, and discuss issues of concern with them. Teenagers have a way of isolating you as the sole "freakish" parent who is unreasonable about curfews, pocket money, and so forth. Don't you remember pulling that one on your parents? Getting to know other parents will reassure you that you know better.

HOW YOU CAN HELP NURTURE THE CAPACITY FOR FRIENDSHIP IN YOUR DAUGHTER

- Accept and encourage her early friendships.
- Invite her friends for impromptu meals and sleepovers, or take them on excursions or vacations.
- Allow her to accept invitations to the homes of friends whose parents you have met (but check by telephone she really is there).
- Be tolerant and recognize her need to move outside the protective home environment, in order to learn about other people and how they live.

It is important to keep in contact with relatives and share family occasions. Cousins make good friends for life. Remind her to send cards and notes to relatives on birthdays and other occasions. A beneficial friendship can be formed with a friend or relative who falls midway between the age of your daughter and you. Such a friend can be an important influence, someone your daughter can confide in over topics that worry most girls, such as attracting boys or gender confusions. Some girls would rather die than discuss such subjects with their parents. Such supportive relationships—including those with aunts or godmothers—can prove a source of strength and comfort on both sides. Don't feel threatened if your daughter develops a friendship like this with an older woman.

Peer Groups and Cliques

Groups or cliques, so dear to most girls, start in elementary school and continue through junior high and high school. It seems that most girls' groups are more concerned with keeping others out and sharing secrets than achieving any particular aim.

Younger girls still in elementary school are usually not yet interested in boys. At that stage, they are likely to view boys as stupid and giggle about them. On the other hand, high school cliques are full of girls who spend a great deal of time talking about boyfriends, clothes and going out together. Some of those girls, who are already sexually involved with boys, discuss their emotions and experiences with their peers or best friends.

During her teenage years, when your daughter is asserting her own identity and moves away from you, she could well feel that belonging to a peer group is very important. Not being part of a group or clique, or not having a "best friend," could lower her self-esteem. Friendships at that age are quite fluid, and she will eventually find a soulmate outside of school, if not at school.

CHAPTER 2

APPLYING RULES AND SETTING BOUNDARIES

Ground rules are there for good reasons. The most important considerations are your daughter's safety and your peace of mind. Your daughter should also learn to have respect for other people and their property.

While the need for rules is obvious to parents, teenagers often regard them as unfair attempts to limit their freedom. If your daughter understands and accepts the reason for a certain rule, a cause of potential conflict is removed. Unfortunately, most teenagers regard themselves as adults, confidently tackling the world, while caring parents are keenly aware of potential dangers.

Rules are more likely to be observed when they are mutually agreed upon. If your daughter is particularly willful, her acceptance of the house rules will make it easier for all concerned. Keep discussions constructive. Encourage her to negotiate if she wants a change to a particular rule. Learning how to get changes by negotiation rather than by confrontation is an important life skill.

Draw up rules that are appropriate for your daughter's age and commitments and modify them as she gets older. Check with parents of your daughter's friends to find out what arrangements they have arrived at if you are uncertain.

Be flexible. Take into consideration that times have changed since you were a teenager. Students are often expected to take part in extracurricular activities organized by various groups. Before the beginning of the new school year, find out how these may affect her study time. Also consider her safety, if she needs to use public transportation to attend such activities.

Disagreement between parents on points of discipline or rules will encourage your daughter to shop around for the decision she wants. Resist her attempts to wangle a favorable decision by playing one parent against the other. Being seen as "a soft touch" could lead to great discomfort for either parent and could have repercussions.

Check with your partner if you have any doubts about a particular request. Involve your partner in important discussions with your daughter, and, if possible, refrain from contradicting or overriding each other in front of her.

When Rules Are Broken

Your daughter can give you a hard time by simply ignoring previously negotiated house rules when it suits her. Punishment rarely works, so is there any point in making rules if she doesn't adhere to them?

Rules have been broken before: It is not the end of the world. Don't let the situation get out of hand—call a temporary retreat to allow tempers to cool, and back off with dignity. Use a cooling-off period to reassess the situation in a less heated fashion. Listen to your daughter, find out why she broke the rule, and then negotiate a solution. Your experience and understanding of your daughter should provide some insight into her behavior.

If you have a difficult time dealing with your daughter's habitual rule breaking, joining a parents' support group may help. You will become aware of the fact that other parents are going through similar ordeals, and they may be able to offer constructive solutions to your particular problems with broken rules. As a last resort, you may look for professional advice. Counseling helps, but if that fails too, you may find yourself in a deadlock situation.

You have gone through adolescence yourself; you know it's only a temporary state, so try to keep things in perspective. Remember, most unruly individuals grow up to be responsible adults. That prospect may be of some comfort to you when your daughter's teenage obstinacy is getting you down. Many risk-taking teenagers give their parents sleepless nights. Only a few suffer the consequences of their reckless behavior and pay dearly, sometimes with their lives. Adolescents learn eventually that they must live with the consequences of their own actions.

Curfews and Responsibilities

It is one thing to impose late-night curfews on your daughter, but making her observe them is another matter. Up to the age of about fifteen, you may still have control by applying penalties (for example, grounding her, withholding pocket money or not allowing her to watch television). But beyond that age, some teenagers are openly defiant and penalties become increasingly ineffective.

Talking to her about potential dangers may not impress an adolescent who has no concept of her own vulnerability. Involve your daughter in drawing up basic rules, which should apply to all family members, including parents. The following are suggested:

* Always require that your daughter leave a contact name, address and phone number when going out in the evening (an erasable board is handy for this).
* Require that she phone home if she will be out after a pre-determined time, for instance after six o'clock P.M. or sunset—whichever comes earlier.
* Be sure your daughter has enough money for taxi fare home and does not drive with anyone who has been drinking.

Sharing Responsibilities

The role of today's women has changed a great deal. Whatever the reason for returning to work—the desire to work for its own sake, family or professional obligations or financial need—the expectation remains that the mother will be the prime caregiver of the family. This often means that Mom has taken on an extra job with little reduction in family responsibilities.

While there is some concern about stress and fatigue among working mothers with very young children, this can be a positive situation for everyone when older children are involved. Some adult supervision will be required up to their mid-teens, but depending on age, children can be expected to take on responsibility for looking after their own things and doing some of the chores. Knowing how to prepare a meal, do the laundry, iron her clothes, and keep her bedroom and bathroom clean are essential steps toward your daughter's adulthood and independent living.

Becoming responsible is not something that happens overnight; it is a maturation process beginning as early as preschool. Whether or not you have a job in addition to your family responsibilities, your daughter is quite capable of helping around the home. Unfortunately for parents, it doesn't always work that way.

CHAPTER 3

FOSTERING NEATNESS

Is Your Daughter's Room a Primal Cave?

You don't have to search too long before coming across a teenager's bedroom that resembles the home of a cave dweller. An academic recently announced that parents should not worry about their daughters' untidiness—what matters is that girls are raised to be loving and caring. Well, he was right, but only up to a point, and clearly he couldn't have inspected many girls' bedrooms. In some girls' rooms one can scarcely see the bed for the piles of clothes, the damp and smelly towels, the assortment of teen magazines and the dirty dishes. Painting materials, discarded school projects made from egg cartons, old boots and shoes and an empty birdcage sometimes add to the clutter.

Be forewarned. As school studies get more intensive and exams loom, your daughter will use these as excuses for not cleaning up after herself. Such excuses will continue throughout grades eleven and twelve and, if she is still at home, through college. One day she will in all probability leave the

If you don't teach your daughter the rudiments of housework and tidiness before she turns fourteen, you may as well hang up a sign: "Abandon hope all ye who enter here." You are likely to end up with a daughter incapable of throwing anything away or tidying up after herself.

family home to share an apartment or house with others. You will have raised a "roommate from hell"—someone with whom no person who actually does housework wants to share a home. Charming, delightful and intelligent as she may be, she won't help with the cleaning up, and her room will resemble a garbage dump or that primal cave, as it did before.

A few trusting parents believe that, when their daughter has to pay rent or a mortgage on a home of her own, she'll change fast enough. In the meantime, they resign themselves to doing all the housework unaided. Other parents put up with the situation for years, then finally snap and retaliate.

How One Mother Dealt with Her Daughter's Messiness

Tired of her teenage daughter's room resembling an archaeological site, with layers of dirty clothes piled on top of each other, one mother threatened retaliation, but did nothing. The teenage daughter (who had a part-time job) claimed she was far too busy working in the local delicatessen to tidy up her room; yet somehow she always had enough time to go to the movies or out dancing.

Finally, after months of unsuccessful nagging, the mother had enough, realizing she was being taken totally for granted. She walked into her daughter's room, gathered up all the dirty clothes lying in crumpled piles on the floor, loaded them in the car and took them to the dry cleaners. When her daughter returned from school she found a neat, clean room. Thinking her mother had cleaned up and done her laundry as usual, she demanded, "Where are my clothes, Mom?"

"At the dry cleaners, dear," replied her mother calmly. "They'll be ready the day after tomorrow, clean and in plastic bags. Your dresses and shirts will be on wire hangers for you to put in the closet. From now on, anything I find lying around will be dry-cleaned. You'll have to pay to get your things back."

The unusual strategy, born out of desperation, worked. The daughter learned the consequences of ignoring her mother's warnings. Her room is now relatively tidy and her clothes hang in her closet.

Of course, this solution is suitable only with girls who have a substantial allowance or a part-time job. Beware of adopting this method unless your daughter has sufficient money to cover the dry cleaning—if not, she may be forced to borrow or even steal money from you to pay for the dry cleaning.

Getting Your Daughter to Become Tidy

Training your daughter to clean up after herself, do her own washing and ironing and learn to cook some simple dishes is essential to prepare her for independent living. Apart from keeping the family home habitable, doing the chores alongside

your daughter can have an added benefit. While you are working side by side on dull and routine chores, something that is
bothering her may emerge quite naturally in conversation and
can be discussed.

We questioned several parents to find out how they managed to get their teenage daughters to help with housework.
The following strategies emerged:

- Give in and do it yourself: About one in every three mothers admitted they had failed—these mothers cleaned their
  daughters' rooms and washed and ironed their clothes.
  Some selfless souls even washed the boyfriends' shirts
  after the boyfriends had been allowed to become household fixtures.

- Give in and engage a house cleaner: You may be lucky
  enough to have a house cleaner once or twice a week, but
  it is amazing how quickly an untidy daughter can create
  chaos around her.

- Make the culprits pay—first version: At a family confer-
  ence Mom announced that there was only so much money
  in the household budget. Because the children wouldn't
  clean up, a cleaning agency would be employed. They
  would lose out, as under this arrangement there wouldn't
  be the money for that trip to Disneyland or that CD player
  or whatever the children wanted so badly.

- Make the culprits pay—second version: If kids have a part-
  time job, which they insist stops them helping out at
  home, they each contribute 20 percent of their earnings
  to pay for a cleaning agency.

- Institute a buy-back scheme: One parent decided to con-
  fiscate all personal items littering the house and lock them

away. She told her daughters they could buy items back at 50 cents apiece, the total to be deducted from their weekly pocket money.

- Create cleaning schedules: Optimistic parents organize schedules, using an erasable board or computerized list with everyone's jobs clearly outlined on it.
- Offer bribes: Motivate your kids through a scheme, similar to frequent flyer miles. As a reward for doing various household jobs, points are allocated to each child. A certain sum of points earns a treat, such as an outing, a plane or bus ticket to see a relative or friend, or financial assistance toward buying a bicycle. Yes, it's a mild form of bribery, but sometimes it works.

CHAPTER 4

PHYSICAL AND BEHAVIORAL CHANGES

All those hormones, including estrogen, coursing through your daughter's developing body produce more than breasts, hips and pubic hair. They bring pimples, moodiness, tears, defiance and swearing. Try to remember what you were like at that age. A model teenager? Reasonable? Responsible? Really? Think again. The teenage years are a period of turbulent conflict with parents, teachers and anyone *else* who tries to set limits to adolescent lives. Behavioral changes include argumentativeness, defiance, disregard of curfews, impatience, irritability and sheer stubbornness—characteristics many adults also exhibit!

Unfortunately, when the physical changes are most obvious and behavior is most challenging, emotional growth is not in step. Emotional maturity develops more gradually and unevenly; hence parents' complaints about the infantile behavior of adult-looking teenagers. The girl who looks like a young woman is still a child in many ways. She can be, at times, a moody, argumentative child.

Diet and the Importance of Balance

A balanced diet will prevent some of the problems common to this age. But good eating habits don't occur overnight, so establishing positive attitudes toward food at an early age is essential. You yourself provide your daughter with an example, good or bad.

Our body shape is as much the result of genes as of the food we eat. Putting on weight during adolescence is normal, with gains in height and body circumference. Gaining weight is not the greatest harm we can inflict on ourselves—being significantly underweight has more serious consequences (see "Eating Disorders").

Teeth, skin, nails and hair—often the focus of girls' obsession—are indications of health and nutrition. If you want to establish good eating habits, don't make mealtime the occasion for family fights. It doesn't help anyone's digestion or advance family relationships. Meals should be enjoyable occasions rather than confrontational. Good ingredients, simply prepared and attractively served in a warm, affectionate environment do much to build positive attitudes to healthy living, food and family.

Physical Activity

Most schools provide a broad program of physical activities, which are designed to cater to a range of interests and abilities.

Unfortunately, when they leave school, many girls stop playing sports, reduce physical activity, put on weight and commence crash dieting. Luckily, dancing is an excellent form of exercise, and energetic dances are the rage. Partners are optional. Even small efforts, like taking stairs instead of elevators, can help.

Acne: A Hormonal Horror

Acne is triggered by hormones (including testosterone—yes, even girls have it) going into overdrive, producing far too much oil in the glands which, in turn, plugs up the pores and turns to pimples or blackheads. Between 60 percent and 80 percent of teenagers will get acne, 15 percent severely. Acne is not caused by rich or fatty foods, though they don't exactly help. Neither is it due to poor personal hygiene. Acne is a fact of life for teenagers everywhere. You should reassure your daughter that this is only a temporary phase. A wide range of acne zappers are on sale at all drugstores because treating acne has become big business. Acne in some teenagers can lead to facial scarring so, if you are worried, have your daughter see her family doctor, who will recommend appropriate treatment. Very severe cases of acne should always be referred to a skin specialist.

HOW YOU CAN HELP TO MINIMIZE YOUR DAUGHTER'S ACNE AND PERSONAL HYGIENE PROBLEMS

Advise her to do the following:

- Ensure her diet contains plenty of fruit, vegetables, protein and carbohydrates, which are the foundation of good health.
- Drink at least six glasses of water a day to flush away unwanted toxins and replace all those fizzy drinks, whenever possible, with water or pure fruit juice.

■ Shower or bathe frequently because increased sweat glands and teenage anxieties will make her perspire far more than ever before. Without a good deodorant, such heavy perspiration will cause body odor.

■ Do not squeeze those blackheads, zits or whatever. They reappear and can cause scars. What is important is to cure the overproduction of oil, the source of the infection.

■ Use a foaming medicated skin and pore wash, obtainable at any drugstore, to control mild cases of acne, although this is not the solution for really bad cases. Morning cleansing is vital, as we all tend to touch our faces while asleep (hands and nails contain germs).

■ Do not use heavy makeup to cover imperfections as it can further irritate sensitive skin and clog up the pores, preventing the skin from breathing and leading to infection. A special drying agent in a tinted cream, sold in tubes by most drugstores, helps hide and reduce pimples to a certain extent.

■ If acne fails to respond to a skin and pore wash, see the family doctor or a dermatologist.

■ Exercise at least three times a week for thirty minutes. Not only is this of benefit aerobically, but it also gives skin a healthy glow. Perspiring opens pores and helps release all that oil, which causes those pimples that devastate the self-confidence of teenagers everywhere.

Breasts and the Onset of Menstruation

Puberty for girls may start as early as age nine but can begin as late as sixteen or seventeen. The average age for the start of periods is now twelve years and nine months. Girls who exercise strenuously, play lots of sports or are involved in other strenuous activities often start menstruating later. If your daughter hasn't menstruated by sixteen, take her to your family doctor.

The first signs of puberty are enlarged nipples and the growth of pubic hair. Pubic hair growth often starts as young as ten or eleven, and breasts start mounding slightly later.

Your daughter may be embarrassed by her developing breasts, if she is physically ahead of her friends. She may attempt to cover budding breasts by wearing baggy T-shirts or by slouching. Reassure her that her breasts are a sign of approaching womanhood and her future ability to nurture children. Encourage good posture.

Girls who mature later than their friends often fear something is wrong with them. They need understanding and reassurance from parents and good advice. Your daughter's breasts will continue to grow until she reaches sixteen or seventeen. Breasts may be rounded or conical, and the shapes of nipples vary. Other changes at puberty are an increase in height and weight. Hips get bigger with a buildup of fatty tissue around the pelvic area—a natural preparation for bearing children.

In addition to changes to her body, your daughter also has to cope with new and often disturbing sexual feelings. There will also be increased demands in her high school studies. No wonder tempers flare and she has confrontations with you and other siblings.

Your daughter may now start to withdraw from the family. This doesn't mean she is rejecting you—she's just growing up. She needs time alone in her room to look at herself in a mirror and worry how she can ever look like those skinny super-models or Barbie-doll actresses seen as role models by teen magazines. She desperately needs your reassurance that she looks attractive. These huge hormonal and bodily changes mean that your sunny-natured little girl is now prey to gnawing insecurities. Even the slightest criticism of her clothes, her hair, her appearance, her friends or her schoolwork can provoke a stormy outburst, ending in tears.

We stress again that your daughter's moodiness and self-doubts are mainly hormonal, all part of her slow, painful progress to independence and maturity. For parents who have done everything possible for a much-loved daughter, this can be a difficult time during which they are bound to feel hurt and rejected.

Adolescents can become even more unruly if their parents (whether living together or separately) are not united in their approach and so enforce *different* rules and curfews. Arguing will not get you very far with a moody teenager, nor will chastisement. When you feel yourself losing your temper, do *not* enter into a shouting match with your daughter. Instead, walk out of the room and discuss the matter once you have both calmed down.

Even before the onset of puberty, give your daughter a brief talk on menstruation (*menses* meaning "month" in Latin). Explain in simple language that she will soon have a *regular* monthly discharge from the uterus, which will consist of blood vessels and tiny pieces of the lining of the uterus. A single human egg will be released each month by one of two ovaries and travel down the fallopian tube to the uterus. If the egg is fertilized, it becomes embedded in the uterus' cushioned lining and a baby develops. If unfertilized, the egg, the cushioned lining of the uterus and additional blood vessels dissolve, then trickle out through the vaginal opening as a reddish discharge. After a couple of days this becomes reddish-brown. Period pains vary in intensity, and intervals between them can be anywhere from twenty-two to thirty-five days. Most last for five to six days.

HOW YOU CAN HELP TALK ABOUT MENSTRUATION

- Don't put it off. Talk about menstruation before it happens. After her monthly periods arrive, your daughter may turn secretive and flatly *refuse* to talk about sex and reproduction. Find the right moment and have a quiet talk, *not* a lecture. Show her some sanitary pads and tampons and explain how they absorb menstrual fluids. Warn her to change her tampon at least every six hours initially and never use one if the outer wrapping has been broken or damaged as a precaution against toxic shock.
- Tell her, "As you'll be getting monthly periods soon, it's important you know what to do. If you use a pad, it must be changed at *least* three times a day when bleeding is heavy. Some, but not all, authorities recommend using a sanitary pad rather than a tampon at night."
- Let your daughter know that her skin glands will change after puberty. It's good to use deodorant because the skin glands in her armpits and groin are perspiring more and could cause body odor.
- Don't be gloomy and serious when discussing menstruation. In tribal societies women celebrate menstruation with dancing and singing, seeing it as breaking through

the barrier between childhood and womanhood—not something unpleasant.

- Prepare your daughter for what to do if she is not at home when her first period starts. She should place a thick wad of toilet paper in her underwear. If it happens at school, she should go to the school nurse, who will give her a sanitary pad to wear.
- Reassure her that during her periods she can swim, dance, run, exercise, wash her hair, shower and, of course, take a bath.
- If your daughter's periods are very heavy or last more than six days, or if she has "spotting" in between, take her to a doctor. Many girls prefer to see a woman doctor when it comes to discussing intimate matters.

Premenstrual Stress

Adolescence for most girls is marked by exuberant energy and loads of activities at school. This awakening to life's possibilities and the need to study can lead to overtiredness, with far too many activities crowded into a day. Lessons, sports, extracurricular activities and after-school commitments, as well as homework and part-time jobs, eat into time and energy. The result is that in the week prior to the onset of a period, your daughter will be overtired, stressed, easily upset and generally difficult—all ingredients for a family argument.

CHAPTER 5

SEX

Sexually Explicit Media

Girls today are very aware of their developing bodies. Various teenage magazines, like *YM* or *Seventeen*, which have a candid approach to the subjects they cover, are written exclusively for a pre- and early-teen audience. They write freely about dating, sexual behavior and the risks associated with both. Some parents find the explicitness of today's teenage magazines worrying, though editors have begun to take a more socially responsible tact by warning teenagers about the dangers of HIV-AIDS, sexually transmitted diseases and unwanted pregnancies, written in everyday language girls can understand. Some issues have given very sensible advice and stress one important fact often ignored by teens: that talking will bring you far closer together than sex ever will.

Magazines like *Cosmopolitan* and *Glamour,* however, examine material that is clearly inappropriate for a younger audience. These magazines deal explicitly with sexual technique and orgasms, and many parents find that this can send the wrong message to their children. Though the marketing of these magazines targets an older readership, they can easily find their way into the hands of a young reader.

Your daughter is growing up in an era when sex is widely exploited for commercial purposes. She can see sexual content every day on television, video and film. It is sensible to view adult programs with her and use the program as a basis for discussion of issues raised.

Discussing Sex, Vaginal Infections and Contraception

Family practitioner Dr. Jean Sparling says there is evidence that girls who receive the most information are those least likely to develop dangerous sexual habits. She stresses from personal experience in general practice that the emphasis on safety for girls has changed from the need to avoid pregnancy to the very real dangers of sexually transmitted diseases and violence. Remember, AIDS and hepatitis B can kill!

"Children will absorb knowledge about sex from points outside the home if *you* don't talk about it," Dr. Sparling says. She adds that the importance and limitations of condoms should be pointed out to the adolescent just before the onset of puberty, which may now be as young as eleven. It *must* be firmly instilled in your daughter that her body is to be respected by her and *everyone else* with whom she is in contact.

When you discuss sexual matters with your ten-year-old daughter, it is not necessary to discuss foreplay or oral sex, unless she specifically asks about them. But you should make sure that you discuss not only what happens to her body at puberty, but also other issues associated with sexual relationships. These include sexual feelings, sexual behavior, contraception, pregnancy, sexually transmitted diseases and protection from them.

This is the time when girls have sexual fantasies and pin posters of favorite pop or film idols to their bedroom walls. Many go much further. The Youth Risk Behavior Surveillance Survey of 1999 reveals that by their senior year, 65.8 percent of high schoolers have had sexual intercourse; a significant number would have started much younger with 4.4 percent having been initiated into sexual activity before the age of thirteen. If you are shocked, bear in mind that Shakespeare's Juliet was only thirteen when she first had sex with Romeo—as we all know, that relationship, like those of many young couples, was doomed.

The first experience of sexual intercourse for young girls under seventeen is usually unplanned—it happens after a party and may be associated with alcohol consumption (among sexually active teens nationwide 18.5 percent of girls admitted to having used alcohol or drugs at their last sexual encounter).

One positive fact to emerge over the past few years was that 50 percent of sexually active girls were using condoms, a higher rate than in the past, though leaving plenty of room for improvement.

SO, WHY DO TEEN GIRLS HAVE SEX?

■ Young and immature girls often feel pressured into having sex: The boyfriend expects "it" from them.

■ The insecure girl lacks self-esteem and is very afraid of losing her boyfriend.

■ Girls with disturbed home lives are acting out their problems and their desperate need for love and attention—any attention being better than none.

■ The "wild" adventurous girls want to try something new.

■ Group expectation (peer pressure) is that a sexual relationship is included in the definition of having a boyfriend.

■ They are looking for romance, but instead of the love they expected they experience only lust.

Most girls are curious about sex, as they see it everywhere on television, film and video, but they hope for long-term romantic involvement as well. They don't want to sleep around, because they fear that by doing so they could get a bad reputation and risk losing their girlfriends and boyfriend. By tenth grade most girls are beginning to experience estrogen and other hormonal surges and sexual dreams. One fifteen-year-old girl in tenth grade admitted she thought "sexually active" meant kissing a boy behind the bike shed. Once the girl understood the meaning of the word, she volunteered that four girls in her class were on the pill and in relationships.

Substantial numbers of girls on the pill fail to realize that it gives no protection against sexually transmitted diseases (STDs). Some misguided teens are relying on withdrawal as a contraceptive and preventative of an STD, but withdrawal offers no protections against STDs and is only 81 percent effective as a birth control method. More and more teens are turning to the "morning after" pill as a way of preventing unwanted pregnancies after having unprotected sex, and in today's sexual world pregnancy is only one of many concerns. STDs continue to persist in every age group and teens must learn how to protect themselves.

Most sexually active teenagers were aware they could get pregnant from the very first time they had intercourse. They knew the dangers of contracting AIDS and that using condoms was sensible, but most admitted they hadn't insisted on using them. Some girls said they had unprotected sex because they had been too drunk or high to take that precaution. Embarrassment, and not wanting to be accused of promiscuity, stopped girls from buying condoms or getting their doctor to prescribe the pill before having sex for the first time (or the second or the third). The use of contraceptives should be a joint responsibility, but many boys still believe that girls should take care of contraception.

In spite of the sexual revolution, the double standards still survive. For boys, sex with multiple partners is fine, but if girls play by the same rules they're stigmatized. However, if girls say no, in the eyes of many boys they're "teasers," frigid or lesbians. Sometimes girls have sex to remain part of a sexually active clique of girls, or because they believe that male cliché, "If you *really* loved me, you'd let me."

TEENAGE GIRLS' ATTITUDES TOWARD SEXUAL ACTIVITY

- A "nice" girl can have sex, but only with one boy who "loves" her. She cannot change partners frequently.
- Girls monitor each other's conduct closely and can drop any girl from their group who is seen as a "slut" or "wild girl," even if the girl was pressured into having sex.

Falling in Love

Be prepared for an emotional roller coaster if your teenager does fall in love. Teenage love is just as intense, romantic, idealistic and devastating as love in older couples. Nevertheless, many adults think school kids are too young to be truly in love.

Of course you will be protective of your daughter and wary of her boyfriend's intentions. For your daughter's sake, respect their feelings for each other; don't be overly intrusive because you fear what might happen. If they intend to have sex, they will find an opportunity. Now it is vital your daughter is adequately informed about contraception and sexually transmitted diseases. You might be happier if she were chaperoned all the time, but that unfortunately rarely happens. When first love coincides with final exams and there is a conflict between spending time together and the need to study, parents must exercise forbearance together with firmness. Remind the lovesick couple of priorities and the need to look together to their futures.

Cultural Differences

Among certain cultures it is not acceptable for a girl to go out unchaperoned with a boy, especially with someone from a different religious or cultural background. *Any* relationship not approved of by the family can have serious consequences. Living in a foreign country with customs that are contrary to strongly held religious beliefs and fearing for their children lead some parents to reject the idea of the daughter having close friendships outside the family circle. The girl's need to assimilate and cope with conflicting pressures can cause great distress to her and her parents—some girls become depressed as a result.

HOW YOU CAN HELP WARN HER ABOUT THE PERILS OF SEX WITHOUT LOVE AND UNPROTECTED SEX

- Society has changed enormously. You may have been brought up to believe teenage sex was wrong, but most girls no longer believe this and do not value chastity. Your responsibility is to warn your daughter of the risks of pregnancy or sexually transmitted diseases and explain the difference between love and lust. Her self-esteem should include her body. Sex without a previously established a loving relationship with her partner shortchanges her and will lower her self-esteem.

- Discuss peer pressure that your daughter may experience from boys and friends at school.

- Should she decide to take a sexual partner, stress that *condoms must be worn every time* to minimize the risks of catching STDs (see chapter on "Sexually Transmitted Diseases") as well as preventing pregnancy. Always check the use-by date of condoms to ensure they are effective.

- Doctors warn that it's possible to catch sexually transmitted infections through oral as well as vaginal sex. To prevent risk from oral sex, special oral condoms or dental dams should be used.

- If she has a boyfriend and you think she may be trying to make up her mind whether to have vaginal sex, it may help to point out that mutual masturbation scarcely raises an eyebrow in today's world, but getting pregnant most certainly will.

CHAPTER 6

BULLYING AND STEALING

Bullying or Being Bullied

Roughly one child in every six undergoes some form of bullying.[1] Bullied children tend to be timid, nervous, small for their age and perceived by other kids as being "different." They may have a stutter or speech impediment, have a "funny" or foreign name, wear shabby or unfashionable clothes or be bad at sports. Some bullied kids are really square pegs in round holes. A good example of this is academic girls who have been sent to sports-oriented schools, where other kids despise them for being the teacher's pet. Bullies tend to blame their victims, offering feeble excuses for picking on victims like, "It's all their fault. They look odd, wear funny clothes, speak wrong."

Girl bullies can be just as bad as boys; their tactics can include hair pulling, scratching of faces and destruction of schoolbooks. The victim may be locked inside a room; have

[1]. Study on bullying in schools published March 1998 by Dr. Ken Rigby, University of South Australia, and Dr. Phillip Slee, Flinders University, South Australia. See also Dr. Ken Rigby, Bullying in Schools.

clothes, school bags or possessions stolen or damaged; or receive unsigned "hate mail" or cruel drawings.

A great deal of bullying by girls is psychological. The victim, who feels unable to defend herself, is rejected, jeered at, taunted and teased. Another form of victimization is being given the silent treatment, which means that a group of children will not speak to the unfortunate girl. Public rejection by a popular group or clique, which the victim openly or secretly longs to join, can damage self-image and confidence. Such pre-teen and teenage cliques foster close friendships with warm embraces and shared confidences. Girls have an intense need for sharing experiences with a best friend, although such intense relationships often shift and break down over time and new best friends are sought.

A bullied girl can find herself rejected by class members for reasons that seem trivial to adults: having buckteeth, braces, acne or fuzzy hair; lacking the right clothes or sports equipment; or wearing the wrong brand names. The victims may be tripped up or made to stand at the back of the line, ridiculed or called unpleasant names. Parents are frequently at a loss when their child pleads with them not to make things worse by telling the school authorities. The victim fears that there will be reprisals if they "tell"—although this is the best course of action, as bullies thrive on making threats and engendering fears. Older children who bully sometimes demand money, forcing their victims into stealing to "pay off" their assailants. Victims receive lower grades at school when bullies destroy or damage homework, especially projects that have taken many hours to complete. Often several children under an aggressive ringleader pick on one child, making the bullied child's life a nightmare.

Most schools have changed their approach to bullying, which was once thought to be part and parcel of school life. Today in these schools, complaints by parents are treated confidentially. One member of the staff—a department head, the vice principal or a guidance counselor—is nominated as the person to deal with bullying, rather than leaving it up to the victim's class teacher, who may well be young and relatively inexperienced in dealing with the problem.

In many schools the incidence of bullying is being lowered by parents and teachers working together to isolate and punish bullies. At class meetings bullies can be named. In some schools bullies are "outed" in front of their class to release their hold over others, made aware of the effects of their behavior and isolated at recess. Recommendations can be made for counseling or for psychological treatment, or in severe cases the bully can be expelled. "Buddy" systems, where an older child is appointed as a younger child's mentor, have worked very well in reducing or even stopping the incidence of bullying.

Detrimental Effects of Bullying

Bullied children often complain about feeling sick or having abdominal pains before going to school. They can have nightmares and eating disorders, and bed-wetting may become a problem. Victims can become so depressed that some have contemplated suicide as a way out—a small number, suffering problems at home as well as at school, have succeeded.[2]

---

2. Teenage suicides have implicated prolonged bullying at school, usually coupled with severe family problems at home.

Danger signals by depressed adolescents contemplating suicide range from talking about death and giving away prized possessions to failing even their best subjects at school.

Being bullied can have long-lasting effects on the victims' health—both physical and mental. Children constantly teased or isolated by classmates in their early and preteen years show poorer mental and physical health during the final years of school.Overweight girls, teased and given nicknames like "Fatty" or "Thunder Thighs," often start crash diets or fasts that can develop into anorexia or bulimia. Children with names that sound "funny" (and children include foreign names in this category) are often teased unmercifully. Parents, together with the child's class teacher, should try to build up the victim's self-esteem and help her to become more assertive. In some cases it helps if the victim is taught to "walk tall," answer back clearly and, if her voice is high and squeaky, to deepen it.

The victim should pretend not to care but answer threats of violence by assuring the bully that, if it continues, she will tell her parents, who will report her (or him) to the school principal.

How to Beat Bullies: One Family's Story

Klaus Strumpf came from Germany to set up retail outlets for his company and brought his wife Christina and his young daughter Angelika with him. Although the whole family had taken intensive English classes before leaving Germany, Angelika had trouble understanding people. Her classmates at the local elementary school laughed at her "funny" foreign accent and what seemed to them her equally "funny" name.

As Angelika loved learning, she wanted to do well in class and was desperately eager to fit in. But she found herself isolated in a school where athletes were idolized. She no longer received good grades, and she began to dread going to school. All the other girls had friends or were part of some group, but Angelika had no one. She was never invited to other children's homes or parties. She became withdrawn and miserable, but she said nothing at home, as she didn't want her mother to make a fuss, fearing that it would worsen the situation.

Just before her last term, Angelika came home with her schoolbag damaged and her textbooks torn. She revealed that her classmates had teased her unmercifully. They had laughed at her because she could not swim and was afraid of water. Angelika burst into tears and said that she wanted to go back to Germany.

Recognizing that Angelika had a problem, Christina arranged private swimming lessons and, slowly, her daughter overcame her psychological fear of water. Once she had learned to swim she became more self-confident.

Before Angelika started secondary school she met Melanie through church. Having just moved to town, Melanie was also apprehensive about being "a new girl." Christina invited Melanie to her house for tea, so Angelika had a friend before they both started junior high school. The two girls got along well together. They were both interested in music and singing.

In high school, Angelika found herself allotted to the care of an older girl in a higher class as part of the "buddy" system. This time she fit in well, as it was a far more academic school.

Now, two years later, Angelika speaks fluent English and is always near the top of her class. Her talents for music and singing have been recognized, and she is enjoying her new life. Angelika and Melanie remain best friends and have both been picked to tour with the school choir.

HOW YOU CAN HELP YOUR CHILD
WHO IS BEING BULLIED

- If you suspect your daughter is being bullied, but she denies it, watch for torn schoolbooks, bruises or scratches and damage to clothes or other personal belongings. Danger signs can be loss of appetite, stammering, nervous tics, bed-wetting, nail-biting, sleepwalking, sleep-talking or frequent loss of lunch money or her packed lunch. She may come home hungry and conceal the fact.

- Once you are convinced she is being bullied, reassure her that it is in no way her fault. This is vital to raise her self-esteem. Remind her she is a terrific kid, and praise her often. Make her more assertive by role-playing. You should assume the role of a bully and coach her how to respond appropriately.

- Contact the vice principal or the class teacher to find out which staff member is responsible for dealing with bullying. Don't get upset. Request information about whether other pupils are being bullied by the same child. If necessary, present any evidence, such as photographs of injuries or damaged property. The school will investigate and deal with the matter, which is now acknowledged as a serious problem in schools. In severe and persistent cases bullies will be isolated from their classes or sent for counseling. They could, in severe cases, be expelled.

■ Encourage your daughter to get involved with a sport, with music or with any other activity she enjoys, so that she can develop friendships with children who share her interests and so that she is viewed by her classmates as being good at some activity.

■ If your daughter's problems are not being addressed, clearly she is not at the right school for her. She might benefit from being moved to a smaller private school. Montessori or Rudolf Steiner schools have helped in some cases.

Shoplifting Means Stealing

Some girls steal because they are troubled; others do it for kicks. Like adult shoplifters, children often steal what they perceive could (in a distorted way) replace a vital element missing from their hearts and their lives. Others steal to keep up with their group or clique. Some girls steal because they are bullied into it: A few, like some adults, feel they have the right to take what they want. Stealing from shops or homes by teenagers can indicate a drug habit. By the time she turns seven, your daughter should know that stealing is not like borrowing and will cause big trouble if she is caught.

HOW YOU CAN HELP IF YOUR
DAUGHTER IS STEALING

■ You should have pointed out from early childhood to your daughter the difference between what is mine, yours and theirs. Make her apologize to shopkeepers or classmates and take back in person anything she has stolen. Insist that she give something extra back or do something as compensation to anyone she has wronged.

- Leave money in a jar in the kitchen to act as a deterrent (and take the thrill out of stealing). Require your daughter to write an IOU with her name on it when taking money out of the jar and pay it back out of her own pocket money.
- Open a savings account, however small, for your daughter. Encourage her to save a portion of her pocket money or earnings from a part-time job. Ask her how she would feel if the bank stole money from her.
- If stealing continues, involve school counselors or (informally) ask the police for advice. No one wants their children to grow up with a police record, least of all the police. If one is available, try to join a parents' support group for counseling and support.

CHAPTER 7

BODY PIERCING AND TATTOOS

Journalist Kate Collins has done some research into why teenage girls spend good money (often earned from part-time jobs) having their bodies tattooed and metal objects attached to their anatomy. Although body piercing may distress you as a parent, do not panic if your daughter announces one day she is off to the piercing shop. Collins can see the funny side of what is, for most girls, only a passing fashion.

Once upon a time, "nice girls" got their ears pierced as a rite of passage. They chose a pair of simple pearls or gold hoops, nothing Jane Austen wouldn't approve of. Only Tibetans and Hindus wore rings in their noses, and only sailors wore tattoos.

Tattoos became a high-fashion item around the same time as body piercing. Both are subcultural languages, instantly readable to initiates. If you don't know what a guiche is, or a Prince Albert, go to a body piercing shop and ask.

47

What started this sudden lemming-like urge among teens to turn their bodies into dartboards and colanders? One could blame it on their parents, the sixties generation, for trekking off on the Hippie Trail and dragging home ideas gained in the Developing World. You could also blame Demi Moore and Madonna for getting bored with wearing their bras on the outside and turning to torso tattoos and mehndi, henna body art, as a novelty. Above all, don't panic if it happens; stay calm and look for a silver lining. Try seeing tattoos and piercing as degrees in a learning curve and the passing fads and fancies of teenagers.

Tattoos last longer than mehndi, which are relatively cheap to have painted on but wear off after a few weeks. There are henna transfers for the wrists, which are inexpensive and sold by some novelty stores. They resemble delicate artwork, peel off of a roll, stick to wrists, then fade away.

Tattoos take a long time to apply (and remove by laser). The big risk in both tattooing and piercing is infection: dirty or reused needles, cross infection, hepatitis or worse. If your daughter announces she plans to get a tattoo, don't shout or get annoyed. Sit down with her and ask some relevant questions that will, hopefully, make your daughter think twice— "Are you doing this to please your boyfriend or to demonstrate just how unique or independent you are?"

Tell her that tattoos are expensive to remove (around $1,000 to remove a small one by laser surgery, a cost not covered by health insurance). She should think of the future and the cost of removal. On a teenager or college student, a curling vine or a blue and red dragon twisting around a wrist and arm may seem cute today, but it could be embarrassing in the future. Does she plan to work in a conservative occupation, where she could be forced to hide her tattoo with long sleeves, however hot the weather? If, instead of the dragon, she has her current boyfriend's name and a heart tattooed high on the inside of her thigh, could so intimate a tattoo cause problems if she enters into a new relationship?

Piercing is far less drastic than tattooing and easier to remove. The main types of piercing are nose (septum or nostril, which require different techniques), tongue (high infection risk), navel, eyebrow and bridge (between the eyes). Genital piercing is surprisingly popular—clitoris or labia for girls, scrotum (guiche) or penis (the dreaded Prince Albert) for boys.

Reputable shops—and despite parents' fears, there are many—should use autoclaves and single-use disposable needles. Make sure the person piercing your daughter's body is aware of the risks of transmitting hepatitis B by using contaminated needles. Nipple and navel rings should not be too thin or they can catch on clothes and tear away, causing pain and infection. Use only professional practitioners, no talented friends doing a cheap piercing job in their garages. Legally, your daughter can't get pierced or tattooed without your approval until she's eighteen. Piercing and tattoo shops should have a sign on the wall warning about health risks, such as hepatitis and sepsis, and the legal requirement that for anyone under the age of eighteen parental approval is required by law. Really? Tell that to the growing number of pubescent girls who, despite being barely tall enough to see over the counter, seem to have no trouble at all getting nose, navel, nipple, tongue, eyebrow, bridge, ear or—ouch! yes—even *there* studded with silver, titanium or stainless steel rings, bolts and stars.

Adolescents are the last people to take notice of warnings about legal age limits for anything—from sex to drinking to sticking things into themselves. That's why bars and clubs demand ID. Passing yourself off as older than you really are is a teenage art form perfected by years of getting into R-rated movies; it's a group conspiracy in which unscrupulous piercing or tattoo artists are sometimes happy to collude for hard cash.

However, legal consequences against underaged piercing are strict and rigorously imposed. Generally, a proprietor of such an establishment will demand identification and will often make a copy of it for his or her records. Still, teenagers have found and continue to find their way around such obstacles. Some are pierced by friends or at unofficial establishments, or they manage to locate a fake ID.

Try to take comfort in the fact that what we're talking about here is much bigger than your daughter turning her navel into a flip-top beer can or her earlobe into something that would look right under the bonnet of a sports car. This isn't torture; this is fashion. The bad F word. Peer pressure, cutting-edge hype. An industry with its own teen idol gods and goddesses and media gurus handing down commandments from on high. The Viper Room club in Hollywood and the pages of *Seventeen* magazine make the rules. Parents trying to compete with what Gwyneth or Keanu or Smashing Pumpkins dictate should realize they haven't a hope of succeeding.

Before you start blaming it all on premature weaning or your decision to put your kid into daycare and go back to work, let's take a look at some sobering figures.

Q. Which is the biggest single consumer market in the post-Spice Girls world?

A. Thirteen- to nineteen-year-old girls, of course. In the United States alone, there are more than nine million of them, and many have a substantial amount of money from allowances or earned at after-school jobs or baby-sitting.

Q. What do they spend it on?

A. Consumer goods and entertainment. In the United States, female teenage spending surged 4 percent in the past two years. This is serious consumerism, the kind that makes the cosmetic, fashion, fast food, music and movie industries behave like Dracula in a blood bank. Teens spend up to 122 billion dollars annually.

Q. What is the new market?

A. Tweens, kids between the ages of eight and fourteen, are becoming the newest marketing niche in America. This group alone spent more than thirty billion dollars in 2000. Tweens are embracing more and more teen styles and attitudes at an earlier and earlier age. They are fashion and trend conscious with a voracious appetite for the consumption of whatever is new. Tweens are a retailer's dream—the perfect consumer. They are easily swayed by trends and enjoy a certain amount of disposable income attained either through allowance or odd jobs like baby-sitting or mowing lawns.

So that's why your daughter is hobbling around on her twelve-inch orthopedic platforms that make even Chinese bound feet look sensible. That's why she did that strange thing involving green dye with purple stripes to her gelled hair. That's why she has black nails and bits of metal sticking out of every orifice. It's not that she's trying to get at you. She's just the same entity that you were back in your youth, a dedicated follower of fashion.

The answer to all parents' worries is that what goes in your daughter's body may, eventually, come out or off. By the time your sixteen-year-old turns eighteen, sanity and a more clearly developed sense of aesthetics will, hopefully, prevail. If not, chances are the inserted objects will get infected and have to come out very soon on health grounds. This happened to Kate Collins' child. The obvious discomfort was a joy to watch, a learning curve in stoicism as much as a practical lesson in the dangers of being a fashion victim.

Responsible practitioners will emphasize that the wounds (which are what tats and piercings are) must be kept scrupulously clean with antiseptic lotion and customers must return for checkups afterward. How soon or how often depends on the procedure. If the piercing shows signs of infection, the ring/stud/whatever should be immediately removed and the hole allowed to heal over. Voila!—the piercee has far too many painful memories to go through the whole procedure again.

Infection is a long-term hazard, especially if autoclaves have not been used to sterilize instruments. Even the information leaflets handed out to would-be piercees by professional piercers admit as much. Here are telltale signs of infection she (and you) should look for:

- seepage of pus around the metal
- rashes or blotchy red marks around the piercing

Sounds inviting, doesn't it? It's even more unlikely that the about-to-be-pierced teenager bothers to read the fine-print warnings. If she did, she'd worry that piercings are done without anesthetic.

Doctors and dentists are specific about the inherent dangers of infections. Many dentists particularly dislike tongue or lip piercing, because of the higher risk of infection associated with the mouth. Food and plaque are likely to cause major problems when it comes to keeping any new wound clean in the mouth. Even if the piercing heals cleanly, infection can occur years later, and with tongue or lip rings or studs chipped or eroded tooth enamel is a definite problem. So is the danger of choking should a tongue ring or stud backing come loose and be swallowed, particularly while the wearer is asleep.

The techniques used to pierce your daughter vary for different parts of the anatomy. Experts discourage home piercing kits and insist that piercing equipment should be sterilized in an autoclave. An earring can be inserted using a kind of staple gun. This isn't feasible for the nose, which has much harder cartilage in the septum and nostrils than the ear has. A nose ring requires the use of a special piercing needle, which should come fresh out of its wrapper. So does the nipple pierce. As for the clitoral pierce, anyone prepared to undergo this without anesthetic is likely to be beyond reasoning.

When your daughter announces she is about to get pierced, do not scream at her. Instead, just as you did when she wanted a dragon tattooed on her arm, ask calmly:
* How do you feel about having a large piercing needle or stud gun stuck into you *without* an anesthetic?

- How will you pay your dental bills when your teeth start looking as though you've been chewing beer cans?
- How do you plan to keep from choking to death during the night if the metal stud through your tongue falls out?
- How will you go through the airport metal detector without setting alarms ringing, leading to a full body search?

If sweet reasoning fails, accept the inevitable with grace. Be sympathetic, but keep a close eye on her health: Insist that she continue bathing the pierced area with antiseptic. Hang in there! Remember, all teenage fads have their day, then go out of fashion.

Navel Rings and Daughters: One Family's Story

All hell broke loose during dinner when pretty, dark-haired Sally, two months short of her sixteenth birthday, announced that she had her navel pierced and a ring inserted. Her parents stared in disbelief as she pulled up her T-shirt to confirm what they hoped was a bad joke.

Sally was considerate, affectionate and seemingly unaffected by teenage angst, extraterrestrial hair, black nail polish and so forth. Her parents' first response was reproach. How could she have done something so dangerous, so foolish, so horrible? What right did she have to mutilate her body? It must be removed—immediately!—all normal reactions.

Sally remained cool, pointed to her mother's pierced ears, and reminded her they had agreed three years ago she could have her ears pierced. Sally asserted her right to make decisions about her own body, replying to her parents' question as to the reason she had done this that she liked the look. Full stop!

She assured her parents that she had gone to a reputable place that pierced hundreds of people.

The parents tried the medical danger approach. Was she aware of the dangers associated with these activities: hepatitis, tetanus, HIV infection from needles, dreadful scarring? Sally replied that she bathed the navel every few hours and was following instructions to keep it clean, as she had done when her ears were pierced.

They tried the bullying approach. She had to remove the ring. Point blank refusal. They pointed out that technically she was under the age to give consent and that under law the piercing establishment was guilty of assault, as she was a minor. Her parents informed her they were going to report the matter to the police and speak to the shop owner and their lawyer. Voices were raised. Sally began to cry. The parents thought they were getting somewhere. Then Sally announced that when she turned sixteen, she would leave home and they couldn't stop her.

Things were going from bad to worse. The parents didn't want Sally to leave home. They wanted her to remain at home but without that ring. And here she was saying that she would leave.

Her father said that there didn't appear to be any infection and that was their prime concern. He suggested the "implant" be medically checked and advice sought about potential dangers should Sally contemplate further body decorating.

Sally agreed to have the family doctor check her out and, if there were a problem, to remove the ring. Mother called the doctor's office for an appointment and told the doctor that they wanted the ring removed and Sally given a strong talking to. The doctor examined Sally and explained some of the complications that could arise.

Mother looked grim and insisted he remove the ring then and there. The doctor looked from mother to daughter and asked whether Sally would agree to his removing the ring. This halted mother in her tracks. She had not considered the possibility that removal had to be consented to by her child. Mother insisted that her daughter agree. Sally burst into tears. The doctor, sympathetic to her distress, offered Sally a box of tissues and invited her into an adjoining room where she could compose herself.

While Sally was outside, Mother and the doctor had a quiet talk. He reassured Mother that there was no risk of infection and that the wound was healing well. He also pointed out he was not prepared to remove the ring *without* Sally's consent, as that would constitute assault. He advised the parents to try living with the navel ring until Sally, in all likelihood, removed it herself when she had outgrown the phase.

The parents spoke to the piercing shop's manager about the circumstances whereby a minor had not been asked for identification prior to the operation. The manager insisted that anyone who came in was asked for an ID. She was advised that a complaint had been made to the police (who had referred the matter to the Juvenile Aid Bureau) and that assault charges could be pending. The manager was frank about the problem of minors in her shop and said she could not afford to take the risk of piercing them or she could be sued and closed down. Her problem was that teenage girls' appearances were deceptive: They used ID cards of older friends or even those of their friends' older sisters to establish "proof" of their age.

The local authorities went to the piercing shop and spoke to the proprietors, warning them of the legal risk of not properly verifying identity and proof of age. After talking it over, the parents agreed to take no further action. Sally did not flaunt her victory. Every time they caught a glimpse of the navel ring, her parents bit their tongue. In fact, a tongue ring would have been worse.

It seemed a long six months. Then, one day, Sally's navel ring was no longer there.

CHAPTER 8

FLIGHT FROM THE NEST

Leaving Without Your Permission

Many young girls will run away from home, or discuss leaving home with their friends, in response to what they perceive to be stressful family relations. Some, like the girl in our real-life story coming up, leave because they are sexually involved with a boy of their age. Sometimes they leave home for reasons that do not seem rational to parents. Therefore, it is vital that you listen to what your daughter regards as problems with home and parenting. Try and have a discussion with her at a time that you choose rather than one she chooses. Be well prepared and stay calm, as teenagers can become totally irrational about measures you see as protecting them. And keep in mind that many parents like yourself can sometimes be irrational in an attempt to protect their child.

Beware of those guilt traps into which many girls try to lead parents. You have provided a safe, loving home, food and education. Point out to her quite clearly all the things you have done and which you believe are important for parenting, starting off with the fact that you are the person who loves her most. If she still decides to leave home without your permission, she will remember this when the going gets tough.

Before the age of sixteen, most girls have no idea of the dangers attached to leaving home and "roughing it." They honestly think they can manage alone, leaving parents frantic with worry.

In the United States, the minimum age a student is allowed to leave school is sixteen. Strangely enough from the parent's point of view, there are no hard and fast legal rulings about the age that children can leave home, although under common law (a body of knowledge built up over centuries), judges, when settling disputes, usually indicate children can leave home at sixteen. Be aware that *no* government department or its paid social workers can give your daughter permission to leave home; neither can they force children to return home.

Children often test their parents. Faced with threats of your daughter leaving home, calmly point out that she will find it very difficult now to live on her own. She will also find it hard to get temporary or part-time work. Do some math with her. Show her just how much it costs to live in even the most basic type of rented accommodation. Unlike home, the phone she uses so much will no longer be free; laundry, food and transport will also cost money. Living on the streets is not the answer, as children are routinely hassled there for sex, beaten up or even murdered. Ask her why, if living away from home is so marvelous, these days it has become common for people in their twenties and thirties to return home and live with their parents.

Do Today's Kids Behave Worse than Their Parents Did?

Back in the 1970s, toward the end of the long summer holidays, my daughter Carla, then fourteen years old, wanted to join her older brother and his friend John (at that stage I didn't realize that she had a crush on John) to go grape picking in Mildura. Mom had already agreed. "So it's all right with you too, Dad?" she asked.

I told Carla in no uncertain terms it was not all right with me. I reminded her that she had to go back to school within a month. Carla promised with her hand on her heart that she would be back before the start of school. It took a great deal of persuading on her part, but eventually I acceded to her wish, as long as she kept her promise. " 'Course I will!" promised Carla convincingly.

But when the holidays were over, Carla did not turn up. I felt hurt, angry and let down by my attractive but totally unreliable daughter. Fortunately, I knew from my son where all three of them were staying. My first impulse was to fly to Mildura (a long way from Brisbane, my home), find Carla and drag her home. I agonized all night and then considered it better to send her a plane ticket, accompanied by an urgent request that she return home forthwith.

Four days later a letter arrived from Carla with the plane ticket. "Sorry, Dad, I'm staying with Hugh and John in Mildura."

In despair I consulted the local police to find out what I could do, as Carla was required by Australian law to return to school until she was fifteen. The police officer shrugged, "Why

bother? This sort of thing happens all the time. She'll be back
. . . eventually." I gave up.

Carla returned home after she had her fifteenth birthday
and was legally no longer required to go back to school—something she had no intention of doing anyhow.

The years passed. Carla, now thirty-six, is happily married
and has three children. Justine, her eldest daughter, is receiv-
ing good grades at school and enjoys reading and learning
tremendously.

Recently I reminded Carla of how she ran away from home
when she was Justine's age. I asked her how she would
respond if Justine should behave as she had. An expression of
horror appeared on her face. "Never, never would I allow Justine to do a thing like that!"

The irony is that Justine is determined to go to college and
become a teacher and has no wish to take off from school. It
proves that today's kids are not necessarily any worse than
their parents and there is hope for their future.

Moving Out with Your Blessing (Well . . . Sort Of)

Your daughter is moving out, and she is only seventeen or
eighteen. How well will she cope without you?

This is the ultimate test of your parenting skills and how
you have prepared her for independence. Her reason for leaving could be to study or work in another town, to marry or to
move in with friends or someone special. For the small town
or country child, this transition from living in a close family,

a small community where she is well known and knows everyone else, is a major milestone. Moving to another town or to a big city, establishing a new network of friends and adjusting to life in a college residence or a shared house can be a daunting experience.

Most girls cope well. There is all the excitement of new freedoms, meeting and getting along with a variety of people; managing limited finances; making choices about food; balancing work, leisure and sleep; coping with laundry and cleaning. Your daughter will need to draw on inner strength to deal with loneliness, occasional sickness, decision making about jobs or courses that don't work out and emotional ups and downs. These are survival skills that she has to learn.

Don't worry if your daughter is not good at keeping in touch with you and prefers to go off with friends on free weekends rather than come home. This means you have done well: She has adjusted to her new life.

Your Daughter Moves in with Her Lover

It is very hard for parents to accept that their daughter has moved in with a boyfriend, especially if there seems to be no apparent intention of marrying or making a lifelong commitment.

Parents are still very protective of daughters. They fear their daughter will be misused or her heart broken. Cultural backgrounds can make this situation particularly difficult to cope with. A family's religious beliefs and traditions about the roles of men and women can make it difficult to accept the freedom of choice that women have gained for themselves in our society and the subsequent loss of authority of fathers or father figures.

A parent's relationship with her or his daughter can be either very close or confrontational. There is the temptation to see her decision to leave home as yet another example of willfulness. If parent and daughter are close, it can be very hard to bear the shift of emotional focus away from the family, especially if you do not approve of the boy or man involved. The heart tends to dominate in these decisions: It is risky to force your daughter to choose between him and you. You have to make your decision as to whether she and her partner are welcome. If you accept the situation with grace, you will make it easier for her to return home should things not work out. If you reject her and decide not to condone what you consider to be an immoral or unwise situation, think carefully about whether you would judge a son's action as harshly.

Your Daughter Won't Move Out

Some parents would like their adult children to experience life, be independent, get part-time work if they are students or, if already in the workforce, leave home and start being responsible for their own lives. The parents themselves want to get on with their own interests, travel, see more of friends or move into a smaller house or apartment requiring less work. But what happens? Their fledglings simply won't fly away.

Some cities are prohibitively expensive to live in and, unfortunately for this generation, moving out of a parent's home into rented or purchased accommodation is not nearly as easy as it was for their parents. It seems that anything they can afford is a "dump" that gives parents nightmares.

Even so, although home is comfortable and convenient, there does come a time when young adults have to start earning their way, move out and take responsibility for their own lives. If your daughter is a student, she should be looking for part-time work, either on or off campus. If unemployed, she may be eligible for assistance and should be looking to improve her qualifications.

Encourage your daughter to move away from home by helping during the initial period by giving her household items you don't need and a few groceries. Encourage her to visit regularly for meals and weekends. It is a good learning experience for her to have to budget for items like rent, electricity, phone bills, transportation, food and clothing.

Your Daughter's Boyfriend Stays Overnight

Once upon a time, a young woman who met Mr. Right became engaged and married, after which she moved from the parental home to live with her husband. In the 1970s, a young woman who met Mr. Right moved in with him. Often her parents pretended not to know, "saving face" in front of friends and relatives. Marriage often followed after a trial period or when they decided to have children.

Today, a young woman sees premarital sex as normal. She meets Mr. Right and introduces him to her parents, who invite him to stay for dinner. He stays the night. Her parents pretend not to notice when they both emerge from the daughter's bedroom the following morning. On subsequent visits this is repeated, with the young man often staying over the weekend.

Concerned for your daughter's well being, you wonder about the young man's intentions. Should you assume there is a private understanding between them—something that was once known as a "secret" or "private" engagement?

Now that you have met the boyfriend, you may wish to find out something about his background. You should be clear whether you are prepared to accept a sexual relationship between your daughter and him under your roof. Are you going to treat him as a member of the family? Will you invite his parents over for dinner? Will they become part of your extended family?

Full Nest Plus Boyfriend

Gradually, your daughter and her boyfriend may spend more time at your home. If they are students or unemployed, the prospect of marriage would be very remote.

For all intents and purposes, they would be in a de facto relationship, while living in your home. If you are faced with this prospect, think hard. It's your home and it is up to you to decide whether you want to share it with your daughter's lover.

Parents facing this situation are confronted with unsatisfactory choices. Your values, cultural background and outlook will all have a bearing on your decisions. If you have a religious and cultural background that imposes traditional behavior on women, your daughter's conduct and flouting of parental authority will be painful to you. Remember that women have equal rights and, by living in a Western environment, your daughter has been exposed to different cultural influences and acts accordingly.

If you are happy for your daughter's boyfriend to move in, make sure you set ground rules for joint living and review these rules every three or six months:

- You must be able to maintain your privacy.
- Your daughter and her friend must not depend on you for money. They should have a joint income and contribute their fair share for food and other expenses.
- They must do their share of housework.

One positive side of sharing is that you don't come home to an empty house, your daughter and her friend provide company, and you may appreciate having them around. You are also providing a safe environment for young adults. These days it is far less common than in the past for relatives—grandparents, aunts, uncles or older cousins—to provide a safe alternative to home.

If they are both working, the chances are they will eventually move out of your home and live together. However, if they are penniless students, they will be dependent on parents and unable to afford to move out. In addition, as soon as they enter the workforce, they may have to pay off college loans and all this at a time when previous generations of graduates got married, saved for a deposit on a house or bought a car. Small wonder that today far fewer middle-class twenty-somethings are thinking about marriage, buying homes and having kids.

Today, the decision to leave home is more often made by the young adult than ordered by parents. However, letting go with grace and confidence is proof of good parenting and a way to ensure you all maintain a good relationship. Be prepared for returns home when an affair ends, when a marriage or other relationship falls apart, when a job is left or when money is gone or is being saved for a tour of India, Europe or Australia.

CHAPTER 9

DEALING WITH YOUR DAUGHTER AS A SINGLE PARENT

A difficult situation is when the daughter of divorced parents demands to live with one parent full-time. Complex emotions about possession and jealousy must be addressed by the parent who feels abandoned. Children have a deep need to love each divorced parent, no matter what sins have been committed. If spouses and ex-spouses have reached the stage where they can talk once again, it makes things much easier. Remember, kids may explore the idea of living with one or the other parent but still wish that both parents remain in their lives.

Problems arise when the noncustodial parent seeks to "buy" the child's love with expensive presents and Sunday outings, leaving the other parent with all the routine hassles: the car pools, dental appointments and crisis management of adolescent moods.

Playing divorced parents against each other is a well-known syndrome at which many daughters excel: "But Dad/Mom always lets me do X, Y and Z—why don't you?" becomes a catchphrase. Faced with this situation, the benevolent (usually noncustodial) parent must relinquish the "spoiling" role, or trouble will ensue. Many parents are blind to their own behavior, and it may take an experienced intermediary to present the situation clearly when parenting routines change. It is vital to come to an agreement in advance and talk through issues affecting the child's future.

This Couldn't Happen to Me . . . or Could It?

Bullying and harassment of single parents (and sometimes married mothers) by teenage children (particularly those who are larger and more powerfully built than their mothers) is another late-twentieth-century hazard. This problem is encountered by family doctors, priests, counselors, psychiatrists and many parents' support groups, who attempt to help parents struggling with this relatively new syndrome. As family breakdowns soar and resident partners are frequently away on business, working longer hours to keep their jobs, the mother may be left in sole charge for weeks on end. Teenagers sometimes exploit the situation for their own ends. Often a teenage brother and sister join together to bully Mom.

Girls wound and bully with words, making scathing remarks about Mom's social, verbal and parenting skills. Most parents (single or not) are far too embarrassed to tell relatives or friends they are being bullied and losing the battle over discipline. So parents put up a brave front, pretend nothing is wrong and suffer in silence. These are some issues reported by doctors and counselors over which teenagers harass and bully their parents:

- The right to more pocket money or consumer goodies, with kids claiming "everyone else's" parents provide more than they get. One solution to this is to ask your child to produce six "everyone elses" with phone numbers, whose parents can be phoned for confirmation. It's usually impossible to produce them!
- Demands to relax late-night television viewing or party curfews (because "everybody else" is allowed to, so why can't I?). See above about producing six parents of the mythical "everybody."
- Demands to be allowed to adopt modes of dress, pierced bodies and outrageous hairstyles.
- The right to bring home sleazy kids, whom the parent considers highly unsuitable and has told the child so.
- Taking over the kitchen and living room when entertaining school friends or throwing wild parties where alcohol and/or drugs are available. This sort of behavior, once deemed unthinkable, is now increasing worldwide.

Parental Burnout

In most cases the mother is deeply ashamed, feels it is her fault for "not bringing them up properly" and does not like to tell adult friends or other family members that she is being bullied. Recent studies indicate that as many as 20 percent of families do not have the children's father living with them for long periods, due either to divorce or the father's business commitments; it often becomes difficult for the sole mother to get male support to discipline kids.

We have greatly extended the period of education and training required to assume an adult role in our society, so many kids now stay at home far longer. Before college became widely available and teenage unemployment soared, adolescence was, out of sheer necessity, brief. Fifteen- or sixteen-year-olds went out to work as apprentices and felt they played some kind of role in society, however humble. Today, most stay home until their early or even late twenties. Some leave home and, finding the going tough and goods costing money, ping-pong back, often laden with consumer goods. Others face the unnerving and depressing prospect of never finding a worthwhile job. Some are unsure of the future (consciously or subconsciously) and fear they may never be able to have a lifestyle similar to their parents'. So they demand that you, the parent, buy them the electronic toys and designer clothes and shoes they see advertised. This can lead to parental burnout and disillusionment. Pubescent girls, subject to hormonal imbalance and mood swings, experience fluctuating moods and tantrums. By now they know only too well how to wound their mothers by criticizing their dress sense, blaming them for a marriage breakup, and so on. Kids may have experienced domestic violence in their parents' marriage. Fights between parent and teenager may end up as screaming matches involving pushing, shoving and other violent behavior.

A single parent, feeling guilty over marriage breakdown and the child's bitter sense of deprivation and parental loss, hesitates to blame the child. "Oh, it's just Jan in one of her moods!" is a familiar excuse heard by health professionals. The danger is that in a catch-22 situation, the aggressive behavior sets up a pattern for the future. Working longer hours so you can give more money to the problem child or children is no substitute for your time and certainly doesn't make their aggressive behavior vanish.

HOW YOU CAN HELP DEAL WITH PARENTAL BURNOUT

■ Don't give in to teenagers' aggressive demands just to get some peace; the children's offensive behavior will only escalate. If you give your children everything they want, you may have to work extremely hard to fulfill their demands, and parental burnout could well be the consequence.

■ Require your children to contribute to household duties to lessen parental burnout, which is increasing among parents who desperately want their children to love them. Many do everything around the house themselves instead of requiring their children to help. These parents work hard to give their children vacations, nice clothes, computers, stereos, CD players and videos—all the things kids see advertised and wish to possess. Believing they are doing the right thing, these parents fail to set limits, instill responsibility or apply appropriate punishments, hoping to be "pals" with their children.

■ Don't let your daughter bully you. Stand up for yourself. Talk in a deeper voice than normal, and sound firm (even if you don't feel it). Say, "Every family is different. I am not X's mother. I/we don't do this because. . . ." Adolescents need to know where you, as a parent, draw the boundaries.

■ If you can't cope when your daughter physically bullies you, uses foul language or makes unreasonable demands, contact a relative, friend, counselor or family doctor to support you. If your daughter is out of control and you are at the end of your rope, don't be ashamed of admitting it. You could also find encouragement by joining a suitable parents' support group.

CHAPTER 10

IF YOUR DAUGHTER
IS A LESBIAN

Guess Who's Coming to Dinner

Most parents look forward to the announcement that their daughter is bringing someone special home to dinner. So, how would you react if that special person turns out to be female? When your daughter and her partner exchange long, lingering looks, you realize with a shock that they are in a lesbian relationship.

Your daughter may have harbored secret doubts about her sexual orientation for years, which you probably refused to acknowledge. Many parents do not or even refuse to notice signs that their children could be attracted to those of the same sex or be bisexual. You are now both faced with a turning point in your lives. How you will react is vital. If you condemn your daughter's sexual preference or insult her new partner, you risk a scene that may create resentment between the two of you forever. All your arguments in favor of heterosexuality and a "normal" marriage will not change your daughter's sexual orientation or decrease her feelings for her partner.

Many parents deal badly with this situation and "lose" their daughters for years—some leave forever. How can you keep your much-loved baby, whose photographs adorn your home, part of your family? You may not have known any lesbians until now and may have disapproved intensely of lesbianism as a way of life. You may be dismayed or even outraged. But pause a moment—is some of your shock and outrage based on sheer selfishness? Perhaps you resent the fact that your daughter will never give you grandchildren (although with artificial insemination, there is a chance she might). Your feelings are bound to be influenced by your daughter's age. If she is younger than sixteen, the relationship may be only a passing teenage infatuation or crush. After a while, she and her partner may fight bitterly and break up—this happens in homosexual relationships just as it does in heterosexual ones. After living together, she may realize that a lesbian relationship has the same emotional problems and jealousies as a heterosexual one.

If your daughter is reasonably mature, her love for her female partner is likely to be based on a genuine and lasting sexual preference. She may not have told you (parents are often the last to know), but she could have had lesbian experiences at school. She may have tried heterosexual relationships and found the opposite sex disappointing. In today's world, she will have seen many marriages break down, possibly making her cynical about men and heterosexual relationships. Your daughter's new relationship may also have been influenced by her peer group.

You are mature enough to know that life has many unexpected twists and turns. Your daughter could change her orientation but is certainly not thinking of doing so at this red-hot moment. She may even be experiencing some doubts herself, just as people do when engaged to be married; right now she certainly will not thank you for voicing your disapproval. How you behave here and now will set the tone of the long-term relationship for all of you. It can take years to undo harsh words spoken in the heat of this moment.

If you truly love your daughter and she seems to have found a reasonable partner who makes her happy, look on the bright side—at least she is unlikely to get AIDS from her partner. Loving relationships should be spiritual and emotional as well as physical. With any luck, this is what your daughter and her partner have found. They may have been sharing a house or apartment and you liked her as your daughter's "friend." Don't start rejecting or even hating her now because you have become aware of the truth. If you do, you will create a deep division between you and your daughter.

If her partner seems stable and has secure employment, she may well have a positive influence on your daughter. Although you want for your daughter what you consider best, you have brought her up to make choices, and this is her choice.

A Troublesome Relationship

Caroline, an architect, had been deserted by her husband years previously. He ran off with the office bimbo who, after exhausting his savings, left him. Caroline, bitterly hurt, refused to take him back.

Caroline worked hard to send Harriet, the only child of her failed marriage, to an exclusive boarding school while she built her own career. Harriet was a good student who had a brief episode of anorexia but got over it and was accepted into college, where she studied law. Mother and daughter were close. Harriet always phoned home at least once a week. Initially, she had kept quiet about her relationship with a married lecturer named Andrew. Eventually, Harriet got up the courage and told her mother.

Caroline warned her daughter against having a relationship with a much older and married man with seductive charm. Harriet soon discovered that she was part of a pattern. Andrew had been chasing female students for years, pretending that he and his wife had an "open" marriage. At first he played the role of father figure, enjoying making his students psychologically dependent on him and getting them involved, emotionally and physically. Then, scared, he would break off the affair, explaining to the girl in question that it was 'for the sake of his children." When he broke up with the fatherless Harriet, she became depressed and bitter about the opposite sex and never seemed at all interested in any of the "nice young men" to whom her mother introduced her.

One Christmas Harriet came home with an older woman named Wendy, with whom she worked. They both wore identical black leather coats and gold rings, announced they were deeply in love and that they were buying a house together.

Caroline had suspected *something* for over a year. However, suspecting is one thing and finding out is another. Her initial reaction was one of shock and dismay.

Her daughter was in her first year of paid employment. Would her avowed intention to flaunt her gender preferences damage her career? How could she know at this age that she would never change? Caroline voiced motherly concerns. Wendy flew into a violent rage. Harriet, bitterly hurt, told her mother she was bigoted and old-fashioned. Christmas lunch was a disaster. Wendy enjoyed trying to shock Caroline by boasting how she and Harriet spent Sundays in bed together, reading newspapers, making love and doing the rounds of gay and lesbian bars and clubs, the only places where they felt accepted.

In the end, Harriet and Wendy packed their suitcases and departed. For a year, Caroline heard nothing from her daughter. Then one night, out of the blue, Harriet phoned her mother. She told her that Wendy, who had always been very fond of frequenting gay bars and had a drinking problem, had crashed her car while very drunk. It was clear that Harriet was experiencing all the problems found in an alcoholic, violent marriage: jealousy, bitter recriminations, accusations of unfaithfulness, tears, more recriminations.

Eventually, Wendy left, flatly refusing to pay her share of the mortgage, leaving phone and heating bills outstanding. Harriet was distraught by the breakup and could not pay the bills. She called her mother for advice. Caroline's lawyer informed her that Harriet had no legal rights in a lesbian relationship and was not protected by the law. Finally, after Caroline had paid large legal bills, some money was recovered. Harriet sold the house and moved to a rental apartment.

Harriet still goes to gay and lesbian clubs and bars. She has a network of friends, at present no one special, but she is hoping to find a more stable lesbian relationship. Caroline frequently flies out to spend weekends with Harriet. These weekends are now pleasant and companionable for both of them.

Caroline is at heart a romantic. She still hopes that Harriet may find a "nice man" to marry and have children, but she realizes in her more logical moments that this is unrealistic. Caroline now has heart problems and is thinking of retiring early. She knows that her life may be limited. In the years that remain, she hopes to see Harriet a great deal and have as good a relationship with her and any new (and hopefully more suitable) partner. If she wants to continue seeing Harriet, and enjoy spending time with her, it is no good moralizing or disapproving of Harriet's chosen way of life.

A Successful Relationship

Alex and Margaret are deeply religious. They have a daughter named Sandy and a son named Clive. Alex is an accountant, and Margaret works part-time in a restaurant.

Sandy had a troubled school career with a crush on an older girl. She attended college but dropped out and went to live in a commune, which worried her parents. When Sandy left the commune after six months, Margaret helped her daughter move into a rental apartment with another student, Anna, who seemed like a suitable friend for Sandy.

"Bring Anna home for lunch," Margaret invited. Over lunch Sandy told her parents that she had never been attracted to boys. Then she revealed that she and Anna were deeply in love and intended to spend the rest of their lives together. Both parents were horrified and clearly expressed their feelings. Their religious beliefs made it very hard for them to accept Sandy's way of life.

They lost touch for a year. Clive went overseas to work. Margaret and Alex were grieving for their daughter so badly that they decided to invite Sandy and Anna to spend Christmas with them. The girls gratefully accepted the invitation.

Alex and Margaret did their best to make Anna feel welcome. Anna revealed that her parents had refused to have anything to do with her again unless she renounced her lesbian relationship. Over the Christmas period they noticed that, as a result of the relationship with Anna, Sandy seemed more domesticated, more mature and less selfish. Her parents were also relieved to learn that she seemed to have found her niche in life by going to art school. She exhibited her work in shows of gay and lesbian art and designed a float for the Gay and Lesbian Mardi Gras.

Of course, the situation remains less than perfect. Margaret, influenced by her religion, cannot accept Sandy's way of life as being "normal," which annoys Sandy, who desperately wants her mother's approval. Sandy's macho brother Clive, a plumber by trade, is even more disapproving than his parents, so Sandy refuses to speak to him.

Fortunately, Sandy and her parents have a better relationship now: The wounds are healing. Sandy and Anna are definitely an item, and Anna is talking about having a baby by artificial insemination. They have promised to visit Margaret and Alex on a regular basis, and Sandy takes the time to phone home each week.

HOW YOU CAN HELP WHEN YOUR DAUGHTER TELLS YOU THAT SHE HAS A LESBIAN RELATIONSHIP

- It may be hard for you to accept, but try to appear tolerant. Telling you has not been easy, yet your daughter has been honest. Hopefully, she understands that her revelations are hurting you deeply. If you feel distressed, don't show it. It will only make things worse.
- Bear in mind that your daughter's love for you has not diminished. Tell her that you, as parents, love her just as much as before and that you understand the depth of her feelings. Reassure her that she is still your daughter— nothing will change that.
- Don't force your disapproval of lesbianism onto your daughter. It's too late. All you can do now is hug her and accept her as she is. She wants you to like her new partner.
- Reassure your daughter that she is welcome to bring her partner home, just as long as she respects the rules of your house.
- After you have reassured your daughter, point out gently and firmly that you are being adaptable and open-minded. In return, you expect your daughter to be the same. You must both leave lines of communication open. She may have had years of self-doubt and unhappiness; for her to think that her gender preference could ever change is unlikely. Like a new religious convert, she wants to talk in glowing terms about her new way of life and the friends

she has found. She thinks in a new way and will not be prepared to believe anything different right now.

- Be positive. Look for the good points in your daughter's partner. She must have some, or your daughter would not love her.

CHAPTER 11

TEENAGE PREGNANCY

Why Does Teen Pregnancy Happen In the Age of the Pill?

The United States has the highest teenage pregnancy rate of all developed countries. Close to one million American teenagers become pregnant each year, and 95 percent of these pregnancies are unintended. According to Youth Risk Behavior Surveillance Report and data collected by the Centers for Disease Control and state agencies, 42.6 percent of girls in grade 10 (aged fourteen and fifteen) are sexually active, and by the time girls reach grade 12 (aged around sixteen or seventeen) more than half (65.8 percent) of them are having sex. Only about half these sexually active girls reported condom use, while 20 percent reported birth control pill use.

A strong denial factor about teen sex exists among middle-class parents. Most insist their daughter is not interested in boys or if she goes out with them is so responsible that she wouldn't have sex. Many parents repeated, "Yes, I know that X has sex, but my daughter isn't like that." If they discover that their daughter is pregnant, it's red faces and Prozac all round. They fail to understand that the vast majority of teenagers today see no moral value in chastity and feel no guilt about premarital sex.

Few teen girls are aware of the lethal nature of hepatitis B. Substantial numbers of them use no contraception at all and drink quantities of alcohol before having sex, so it's not hard to understand why they become pregnant.

The whole topic is complex: Many different factors are involved in today's rate of school-age pregnancies. In her professional capacity, Dr. Janet Irwin saw many cases of young girls becoming pregnant. After studying the problem for some years, she now believes the main factors for school-age and student pregnancy are these:

- Sheer ignorance. Obviously not all schools (and parents) provide enough sex education, or else the message fails to sink in. Dr. Irwin once had a pregnant patient who had been trusting enough to believe she could not get pregnant as long as she "did it" standing up.

- Contraceptive failure. Most manufacturers point out that their pills should be taken at the same time each day for maximum efficiency. If your young daughter is in a sexual relationship, it is vital that you or her family doctor warn her that all brands of the contraceptive pills can fail to prevent pregnancy due to impaired absorption, prolonged vomiting (which means the gut lining fails to absorb the pill) and/or diarrhea (which causes the same problem). Certain types of antibiotics interfere with the flora that line the gut, which can then prevent absorption of the pill and lead to pregnancy. There are also numerous cases of plain, simple forgetfulness with the pill. In addition, sex with multiple partners is now a dangerous pastime, and the pill gives absolutely no protection against life-threatening hepatitis B, HIV-AIDS or other sexually transmitted diseases.

Condoms can burst or come off during vigorous intercourse, or if they are used incorrectly.

- Risk-taking behavior. This is seen in teenagers who drive far too fast, take drugs or binge drink "for the hell of it" or to act out against their parents. Some young risk-takers have multiple sexual partners.

- Denial—the "it-may-happen-to-others-but-it-won't-happen-to-me" syndrome. For a variety of reasons, teenage girls often fail to use contraceptives when having sex for the first time. Then they start a steady relationship and demand the boyfriend use condoms. Eventually, one or both partners become blasé and feel that while others might, she won't get pregnant.

- An overwhelming need for love—the "I-desperately-need-someone-to-love-me" syndrome. Some girls feel that a baby would provide closeness and satisfy their emotional needs—acting as a "living doll." These girls are usually emotionally underdeveloped.

- A self-fulfilling prophecy. One student proudly told Dr. Irwin, "My mom always says that if I get pregnant, she'll look after the baby." The result of this statement, oft-repeated, was that the daughter obliged her mother. Dr Irwin questioned, "Whose need was it to have a baby—the mother's or the daughter's?"

- Rape. A girl may have been raped or consented to intercourse while under the influence of alcohol, sedatives or other drugs.
- Forceful and/or unreliable sex partner. A girl may not be able to convince her male partner that he must use a condom, or she may fall for his assertion that it may damage or hurt him if she makes him stop. Many pregnant girls counseled by Dr. Irwin told her how they were foolish enough to believe their partner when he promised to withdraw in time (using the technique known as coitus interruptus). Many inexperienced males do not know how to use a condom correctly.

What Can Parents Do to Prevent Pregnancy?

Children today obtain information about sex from various sources other than parents: friends, teachers or community-based sex education programs. Casual sex, portrayed in film, television and magazines, has played a huge role in encouraging high-risk sexual behavior in our society. It's rare today to see a film that does not have a portrayal of sexual intercourse, but condom use is hardly ever shown. Have you ever seen a single female character in a film, at the point of having sex, say, "Suppose I get pregnant? Hold on; let's use a condom"? Condom use for health as well as contraceptive purposes does not encourage young people to have casual sex. Teenagers do not say to each other, "Wow, here's a condom; let's use it to have sex."

Remember, parents and daughters can find it difficult to discuss intimate sexual matters after puberty. You should regard sexuality as a normal part of life and have an open and honest attitude, which you communicate to your daughter from a young age. With so much emphasis in the media on sex, especially in teen magazines, long before your daughter becomes sexually active, warn her she must insist always on the boy using contraceptives to protect herself against sexually transmitted diseases. You may also discuss taking the pill with her doctor.

What Are the Options for Pregnant Girls?

Most pregnant girls find it hard to tell their parents, feeling they have let them down, fearing parental rejection or punishment. One clergyman's daughter told the truth to her hairdresser and her school friends but could not tell her parents, so she ran away from home. You may suspect that your school-age daughter is pregnant when she becomes moody and tense. Then in tears she reveals she has missed one or two periods. Always remember, there is no single perfect solution to this stressful situation. All possible decisions have outcomes that will cause grief at one stage or another.

A "shotgun" or forced wedding is seldom seen as acceptable today. A distressingly small proportion of teenage fathers stay around after the child is born. Any pregnant girl and her parents have very serious decisions to make about her life, her future and the future of any child she bears. She has to find answers to many difficult questions and consider all options.

Provided religious principles are not violated, abortion is one possible solution, or adoption. There will be strong feelings on all sides about what to do: Relatives may offer different solutions. The final choice must be hers, made in a context of calmness and support.

DIFFICULT QUESTIONS TO ASK IF YOUR TEENAGE DAUGHTER IS PREGNANT

■ Does your daughter want to keep the baby or does she want an abortion? If she loathes the idea of abortion but doesn't want to raise a baby alone, what about today's type of "open" adoption, where the child grows up knowing the birth mother and adoptive parents, as one possibility?

■ What is to be done if your daughter wants an abortion but you want her to keep the baby or vice versa?

■ Does she have the necessary maturity to cope with a crying baby and sleepless nights or with an active toddler all by herself? If the answer is no, can she rely on your full parental and financial support to help raise her baby? Can she afford to rent decent living accommodations, or are you willing to provide a suitable dwelling, provide transportation for her and her child, baby-sit, help with feeding and toilet training and so on? All this is time-consuming. Do you have the time and the energy to do this at your stage of life?

■ Will keeping her baby put an end to your daughter's education (either high school or college) or her job training and, consequently, jeopardize her future and that of her child?

■ | Fathers often desert young single mothers once the novelty has worn off, leaving them desperately lonely. Do your daughter's plans take this into consideration?

Finding Unbiased Professional Help

Probably you and your daughter will spend anxious hours discussing her problem but fail to arrive at a clear decision, so both of you may need professional help. Where can you find it? Some pregnant girls find their own way to a counseling service without the knowledge of their parents. However, at least one study has shown that 61 percent of underage abortion seekers told at least one of their parents about their abortion, and of those girls who did not inform their parents, all consulted someone in addition to clinic staff. Parental consent is essential in some thirty states if a teenager is to obtain a legal abortion.

If your daughter is in need of professional help, she should go to a sympathetic family doctor or make contact with a women's health center or family planning clinic. It is your responsibility to encourage her to do this. Ideally, the doctor or the agency should hold a multidimensional view, without putting any pressure on your daughter. A doctor or agency that does not consider an abortion as an option can only recommend continuation of the pregnancy and may offer counseling and short-term support. However, such agencies rarely offer vital support after the birth, when the need is greatest for an inexperienced young and single girl attempting to mother a child on her own.

Abortion Resources

Abortion imposed by parents or the father of the young girl's child is likely to have long-term adverse emotional consequences. Remember that an abortion imposed on a pregnant girl because someone else has a problem with her pregnancy is not a good solution. Planned Parenthood provides confidential pregnancy counseling and can be reached nationwide at 800-230-PLAN. The National Abortion Federation can also provide a listing of reputable abortion providers in your area. They can be contacted at

The National Abortion Federation
1755 Massachusetts Avenue NW, Suite 600
Washington, DC 20036
800-772-9100
202-667-5881

Adoption—Her Decision Only

Some teenage mothers do not want to raise a child alone if their parents will not or cannot help. They want their baby to have a stable home and good educational opportunities and realize they cannot provide these. Others, planning a college education, do not wish to raise the child themselves but have strong moral or religious objections to abortion. In such cases, "open" adoption, where the child has continuing contact with the birth mother (or adoption by a married sister or close relative), can mitigate emotional problems for a relinquishing mother. Considering that there are many stable, suitable parents longing to adopt, "open" adoption does present a workable solution in many cases, as long as no one pressures the single mother into it.

Keeping the Baby

If a pregnant teenager decides to keep her baby, she needs to be made aware of all the facts, including the hard work and sacrifice involved in raising a child and how she will need support from her parents for many years. The most important point is that the girl herself feels she owns the final decision, whatever it may be.

CHAPTER 12

EATING DISORDERS

"Help, I'm Fat!": Obesity and Crash Dieting

More than five million Americans suffer from eating disorders, and more than 50 percent of teenage girls have dieted and continue to do so. A national survey of eighth- and tenth-grade students found that 32 percent skipped meals, 22 percent fasted, 7 percent used diet pills, 5 percent induced vomiting after meals and 3 percent used laxatives to lose weight. These girls lose weight as their bodies employ defenses that humans have used throughout history to counteract effects of famine; they hoard energy, which turns to fat after they stop the diets. Their systems go into overdrive, and very often they put all the lost weight back on. One in every eight dieting girls can develop an eating disorder. Anorexia nervosa and bulimia nervosa affect as many as 3 percent of adolescent and young adult females, and the incidence of anorexia appears to have risen in recent decades. ("Guidelines for School Health Programs to Promote Lifelong Healthy Eating," Centers for Disease Control, 1996.)

Girls today are bombarded and confused with conflicting messages about body shape and food. Photos of razor-thin fashion models adorn magazine pages and are pinned up around the walls of girls' bedrooms. Advertisements in the same magazines, or on commercial television, promote fast-food chains, which offer fattening milk shakes, double burgers and larger size French fries. Small wonder some girls, under stress or unhappy at home, become compulsive eaters and either suffer from bulimia or become obese. Like other addicts, the obese cannot help overeating, hate themselves for it, then rush to the fridge to eat "comfort foods" to erase their feelings of guilt and depression. Obesity places the compulsive eater at risk of heart disease and other health problems. It is vital for the future health of obese girls to see a doctor or nutritionist. They can also be helped by well-established diet control groups such as Weight Watchers. Extreme cases, in which obesity presents serious health risks, may eventually have to be hospitalized for procedures as drastic as stomach stapling.[1]

Anorexia and Bulimia

Anorexia and bulimia are obsessions, caused by deep-seated psychological problems. For widely varying reasons, anorexics hate food or feel unworthy of it and embark on programs of self-inflicted starvation. Often perfectionists, they are convinced that when they become thin, true happiness will be

---

1. Treatment for obesity is given in detail in Suzanne Abraham and Derek Llewellyn-Jones, *Eating Disorders* (Sydney and Auckland: Oxford University Press, 1998).

theirs. Anorexia is a very complex disorder with a wide variety of causes. Some anorexics seek to control parents, relatives and friends through food refusal. Others feel guilt over a past event and punish themselves by rejecting food, determined to become skeletally thin. Due to lack of body fat, many anorexics never menstruate, don't develop breasts and can suffer premature osteoporosis because they do not get sufficient calcium. Side effects include cardiovascular disease and vitamin deprivation, which causes mood swings, loss of hair and insomnia.

Reasons for anorexia are as varied as the stories of those who suffer from it. Divorce or death of a parent can trigger an eating disorder. Victims of oral sexual abuse or rape often convert their feelings of revulsion into a hatred of eating, which involves swallowing. Girls suffering psychological problems for any reason at all can become bulimic or anorexic. Today girls as young as ten are being hospitalized for these illnesses.

Bulimics are usually girls with an obsessive love-hate relationship with food. They try to beat fat by dieting or becoming exercise "addicts." When the strain of crash dieting and constant exercising becomes too much, the bulimic finds relief in bingeing on comfort foods, especially ice cream and custard, which are easy to vomit up. Junk foods provide the comfort the bulimic craves in her efforts to obtain release from stress and tension. By now, she knows that consuming junk foods will make her put on weight, so she induces vomiting by sticking two fingers down her throat. Over time, compulsive and frequent vomiting will destroy the natural movement of food down the esophagus. Bulimic vomiting can become a reflex action, which will, in time, damage the sufferer's intestines.

Bulimics are deeply ashamed of their solitary and bizarre vomiting, so they refuse to admit it to doctors, friends and family. Some worry about damage to tooth enamel and lips and switch to herbal or over-the-counter slimming pills containing herbal laxatives. Others take diuretics, which make them urinate frequently. Some bulimics take up to ten doses of laxatives a day, ensuring their bodies do not retain essential nutrients, vitamins or minerals, with disastrous long-term consequences to their bodies and their moods. Finally, bulimics have to seek medical advice when they vomit up blood or suffer crippling stomach pains. They envy anorexics for rapid weight loss but are unable to starve themselves. They need food. Bulimics are usually very feminine and wish to be admired for their looks but hate themselves for their lack of will power and compulsive vomiting.

Anorexics and bulimics can be influenced by media images of supermodels, often being unaware of the fact that many fashion models chain-smoke or are on heroin or cocaine to kill their appetite, which keeps them slim and admired.[2] Bulimia and anorexia are widespread among girls who aim to copy or become supermodels, ballerinas or gymnasts.[3] Chemical imbalance in the brains of anorexics makes it impossible

2. Larry Writer, "Heroin, Models and Drugs, the Fashion with Weight-Obsessed Young Models," *Who Magazine* (May 11, 1998) cites former British model Kate Hatch and the large number of British "smacked out" models said to have "food poisoning." Richard Maberley, Director, London's Select Models Agency says that "for models with an eating disorder heroin is like Christmas because on heroin they feel no need to eat." Such people are terrifyingly bad role models for girls.

3. One in ten ballet dancers has an eating disorder. Suzanne Abraham and Derek Llewellyn-Jones, *Eating Disorders* (Sydney and Auckland: Oxford University Press, 1998) cites anorexia as affecting one teenager in every two hundred with a peak incidence of one in one hundred among adolescents between sixteen and eighteen. Rates for eating disorders in late teenage girls are now as high as 20 percent—a marked rise in the decade of the 1990s for an eating disorder not recorded before 1980, although obviously it existed.

for them to accept how dangerously thin they have become. It is as though they are two people: An anorexic described how "part of me looked in the mirror and said 'Eat,' while the other part said, 'Help, I'm so fat, I must starve.'" Anorexics and bulimics become anemic, depleted of essential vitamins and minerals, moody and hell to live with. A few become clinically depressed, and in a small percentage of cases can attempt or commit suicide.

Professor Suzanne Abraham of Sydney University has successfully treated a large number of girls with eating disorders. She affirms that most of those who receive professional treatment will eventually recover. The treatment is lengthy and the patient will suffer from relapses. Only 5 percent of anorexics will die from complications or commit suicide.[4] Professor Abraham told the author of this chapter the surprising fact that bulimia was identified as a psychiatric syndrome only in 1980. The number of bulimics has soared, but it is difficult to provide exact statistics, as bulimics hide their disorder, often for years. There are many more girls suffering from bulimia than anorexia.

When Princess Diana admitted that she suffered from bulimia, her widely publicized confession gave self-induced vomiting as a method of weight control social respectability among certain young girls who admired the Princess. One such girl, heartbroken by the Princess's death, lamented in the June 1998 issue of *Cosmopolitan*, "No one understands why I was so upset when Princess Diana died. To me she was not a Royal, she was a friend, the only other person I knew who suffered from bulimia."

4. Andrew Morton, *Diana: Her True Story in Her Own Words* (London: O'Mara Books, 1997).

The World's Most Famous Bulimic

As a result of her parents' stormy marriage, their divorce and her motherless childhood, Diana, Princess of Wales, suffered psychologically. She had dreamed of being a ballet dancer but grew too tall to achieve her ambition. Instead she became the vulnerable, shy and blushing nursery school teacher who thrilled the world when she became engaged to Prince Charles.

The princess' bulimia was triggered by Prince Charles' comments that she was "chubby" and by seeing herself on television wearing a blue suit, which she feared made her look "fat and dumpy."[5] Worried about appearing on television at her wedding ceremony and about her husband's fondness for family friend Camilla Parker Bowles, she dieted, released tension by bingeing on ice cream, then agonized about putting on weight. Soon the princess discovered she could gain comfort from eating but still lose weight if she managed to make herself vomit.[6] Using this method she lost pounds by the time of her wedding, where, in spite of her nervousness, she performed brilliantly.

Her main reading material since her schooldays had been romantic novels by author Barbara Cartland (whose daughter became the princess' stepmother). Yearning for a great and passionate love, the princess feared that hers for the prince was not reciprocated, although initially Prince Charles was infatuated with her beauty, her sweet nature and her concern for others. But the stress of being in the glare of publicity left

5. Ibid., p 56.

6. Ibid., pp. 127–131.

her, still an immature young girl, exhausted and nervous. Releasing tension through bingeing on food and vomiting helped her cope with premarriage nerves.

By the time of her honeymoon she was vomiting four times a day. Chefs on the royal yacht were amused when the princess consumed "endless bowls of ice cream," and even asked for bowls of custard to eat in the royal cabin.[7] But always there was another camera to face, another photo opportunity: So she continued crash dieting, interspersed with eating quantities of ice cream, custard and chocolates, then vomiting them up in secret in her private bathroom.

Photographed in Scotland after the honeymoon, she looked skeletally thin. She even fainted when visiting the World Expo in Canada, having eaten nothing but a few biscuits for days beforehand. Her passion for gymnasiums and exercise and her devoted care for others less fortunate than herself were typical bulimic behavior.

Under stress from having to make public appearances and from marriage problems, she binged on comfort foods and took diet pills containing herbal laxatives. Her bulimic behavior and her resulting mood swings gradually worsened. When pregnant with Prince William, the princess gave up personal appearances and stopped inducing vomiting, for the sake of

7. Professor Sir Martin Roth, then head of the Department of Psychological Medicine at the University of Newcastle and president of London's Royal College of Psychiatrists, was for a time providing regular consultations to the royal family, and had she told him about bulimia could have treated her. (The author's ex-husband, a psychiatric registrar, used to cover for Sir Martin's NHS patients when the distinguished psychiatrist went to London to consult at Buckingham Palace. However, bulimics are deeply ashamed of their vomiting behavior, so the princess told no one and went untreated for a decade. It seems unlikely that she could have carried out her public program had she continued to vomit four times a day, instead of relying on huge doses of herbal laxatives, but her self-induced vomiting, according to Morton's book, returned when she stayed at Sandringham or Balmoral, which she found very stressful. It is more likely she remained slim by using huge and frequent doses of herbal laxatives and diuretics in over-the-counter diet pills.

her baby. As a result, her depression and mood swings abated and her former sweet and charming personality returned. However, after the birth she suffered postpartum depression.

Like all bulimics, the princess denied her vomiting behavior, even to herself. For years, she refused to confide in the family doctors or psychiatrists who treated various members of the royal family and so remained untreated.[8]

Bulimics present a sunny, feminine exterior, under which they conceal hurt, deny their problem and channel enormous effort into helping others. Princess Diana became loved and honored worldwide for her work with sick children, lepers, battered wives and AIDS victims and for her role as loving mother. She kept hiding her eating disorder from the public. Her whole metabolism became deficient in potassium and essential vitamins, causing more fits of depression, mood swings and outbursts of jealousy, which worsened as her marriage crumbled and she became even more jealous of Camilla Parker Bowles.

Only after her divorce did the princess, after struggling with bulimia for a decade, seek treatment, following the threat of public disclosure by a close friend, who feared she might kill herself. Finally, the princess consulted eating disorder specialist Dr. Maurice Lipsedge, of Guy's Hospital, London, who made her acknowledge her problem and decrease her preoccupation with food and weight. She kept a diary of everything she ate. She was made to eat sensibly three times a day and release tension by methods other than binge eating and vomiting.[9]

8. The princess was also helped by Suzy Orbach, author of *Fat Is a Feminist Issue*. Several herbalists in London and Australia claim to have reduced the princess' stress levels, but specialist treatment was vital to get rid of bulimia.

9. Princess Diana was, according to Andrew Morton's book, also helped by Suzy Orbach, author of *Fat is a Feminist Issue* and by a Sydney herbalist.

Dying so young, the much-loved princess became the tragic media heroine of the latter part of the twentieth century, mourned by admirers all around the world. She had successfully hidden her bulimia from the public for many years, probably unaware that so many teenage girls and young women shared this eating disorder with her. After the princess had revealed her bulimia in Andrew Morton's book (for which she provided Morton with taped information), hundreds of girls who adored her and tried to copy her glamour and style found comfort in the fact they shared the terrible scourge of bulimia with the glamorous, slim princess.

HOW YOU CAN HELP PREVENT YOUR DAUGHTER FROM DEVELOPING AN EATING DISORDER

- Persuade your dieting daughter that not everyone can look like a supermodel or Barbie doll or should *want* to. Explain that many top fashion models and pop singers are desperately insecure in a competitive world where good looks rule. Such heroines are *very* flawed role models with a short shelf life—why not find others?
- Explain that bodies starved of food start hoarding energy, which turns to fat once the dieter eats again.
- Do not complain about your weight or shape in front of your daughter. It is modeling a bad attitude.
- Pin up photos of well-rounded girls rather than supermodels. Tell your daughter that if you respect yourself and your own body, then men will too. Explain how anorexics and bulimics have foul-smelling breath and can get stom-

ach pains, anemia and fits of depression. Does she really want to join them?

■ Beware if she wails about being "fat" or is frequently tired and moody. She may be smuggling food from the table in a napkin (or feeding it to the dog). See if she makes frequent visits to the bathroom or toilet after meals. Don't be fooled if she takes over the cooking and fusses around in the kitchen, offering food to everyone else. Anorexics frequently do this to cover up the fact that they are not eating.

■ If she needs help, persuade your daughter to see your family doctor, who may treat her or refer her to a psychiatrist or specialist in eating disorders. The sufferer and her parents can also benefit by joining an eating disorders support group. The National Eating Disorders Association provides all kinds of information about eating disorders, including a treatment referral directory and support group registry. They can be contacted at this address:

National Eating Disorders Association
603 Stewart St.
Suite 803
Seattle, WA 98101
800-931-2237

You can also find information and on-line support groups at www.HealthyPlace.com.

CHAPTER 13

TOBACCO: THE FACTS

The Greatest Cause of Disease in the World

In many countries tobacco companies, now seen as marketing death in return for dollars, are banned from advertising in magazines and on television, so they employ spin doctors to insert cigarettes into stage plays, films and magazine illustrations targeted at adolescents. The tobacco companies' hidden agenda is, "Hey, kids! Smoking is sexy, sophisticated and cool!"

Only recently have tobacco advertisements on billboards and television been banned in some countries. The World Health Organization claims that smoking is "the greatest cause of disease in the entire developed world." Cigarette and marijuana smoking are major causes of lung cancer and cancer of the mouth and tongue. Intent on staying slim, many girls choose to ignore the fact that smoking can cause an early death. If girls smoke and diet, and do not take added calcium in milk or calcium tablets, they may get bone fractures due to premature osteoporosis. According to some physiothera-

pists and doctors, this is now occurring in relatively young
women.

IMPORTANT POINTS TO REMEMBER
ABOUT THE HAZARDS OF SMOKING

■ Smokers have fifteen times more chance of developing
lung cancer, eight times more chance of developing heart
disease or a heart attack and are ten times more likely to
die from lung or tongue cancer than nonsmokers. Smoking also contributes to osteoporosis.

■ Deaths in men from lung cancer have dropped, but a
higher smoking rate among women, many of whom use it
to arrest appetite, has resulted in increased deaths in
women. Tar is released from cigarettes in the form of particles in inhaled smoke. Black sticky tar collects in the
lungs, causing cancer. Smoking twenty cigarettes a day
over a year means inhaling half a cup of tar.

■ Smoking is directly linked to gastric ulcers, chronic bronchitis and asthma. In 1997, lung cancer surpassed breast
cancer as the number one cause of cancer-related deaths
among women. More than 150,000 women a year die of
smoke-related illnesses.

■ Second-hand smoke from being in the same room with a
smoker can injure the lungs of all those around the
smoker. Smoke inhaled from the burning end of a cigarette contains more poisons than first-hand smoke. Second-hand smoke harms fetuses and babies in their cribs
and contributes to sudden infant death syndrome (SIDS)
or crib death. In the face of so much adverse information,

Preteens and teenagers are twice as likely to smoke if both parents smoke; they are four times as likely to smoke if parents and older siblings smoke.

it seems incredibly stupid that girls are smoking at an earlier age and in larger numbers than boys.

Why Are Relatively Young Girls Smoking?

Girls who take part-time jobs have enough disposable income to buy cigarettes, and many believe smoking makes them look sophisticated and grown-up. Preteen and teenage girls are highly influenced by their clique or peer group. If your daughter's clique smokes, your daughter, eager to be popular and part of the "in" group, may join in. Most girls in the teen and preteen group want to do exactly what the others do. Smoking often starts at a time when girls reject parents' values and rebel against authority. Smoking is legal, and girls see adults doing it. Adults have heeded health warnings and are now smoking less. However, girls as young as ten or eleven are now smoking, finding it attractive because it reduces their appetites.

IF YOUR DAUGHTER SMOKES, THIS IS LIKELY TO HAPPEN TO HER

MOUTH AND LARYNX
- The risk of very painful cancer increases.
- Teeth are stained.

TONGUE AND NOSE

■ Sensations of taste and smell are dulled.

BRONCHIAL TUBES

■ Susceptibility to colds increases.

■ Filtering action of the tiny hairs that stop dust particles from entering lungs is reduced.

■ Coughing increases.

■ Respiratory infections increase.

■ Chronic bronchitis develops.

■ The risk of cancer is high.

LUNGS

■ Shortness of breath occurs.

■ There is a great risk of cancer.

■ Emphysema develops (loss of elasticity and deterioration of lung walls creates severe breathing difficulties).

NERVOUS SYSTEM

■ Hands tremble.

■ Muscles tense up.

HOW YOU CAN HELP ENCOURAGE YOUR DAUGHTER NOT TO START SMOKING OR TO QUIT

■ Don't smoke yourself and set a bad example. If you can't stop, don't smoke in front of her, and explain that it's a bad habit you would like to quit.

■ Warn her not to start. Nicotine contained in all cigarettes is a highly addictive as well as a deadly poison. At first, the nicotine stimulates smokers. Then, after a while, it relaxes them—producing the "feel-good" effect. Years later it can

> **It is far easier not to start smoking than to give up. Smoking is addictive. Most smokers want to quit when they read about the dangers but suffer from withdrawal symptoms when they stop or cut down their nicotine intake. They feel tense and nervous, develop headaches or eat more. Your daughter needs your support at this time.**

kill them or render female smokers sterile for life. Is she prepared to risk being unable to have a baby later in life or having a baby that is less than robust?

- Tell her that all smokers have foul or "ashtray" breath and their teeth will eventually be stained brown with tobacco. Smokers look much older than they really are, because their skin wrinkles faster and becomes dry and dingy. Smoking tobacco is definitely not something cool or sexy that makes women attractive. Those beautiful color advertisements for cigarettes in magazines showing glamorous young people smoking and frolicking beside pure mountain streams are nothing but lies. The sad and unglamorous truth is that smokers are blackening their lungs with sticky tar. Many will die prematurely from cancer and other diseases or spend years and years coughing up phlegm.

- If your daughter is earning good money from a part-time job, encourage her to save for something worthwhile rather than fritter the money she earns away on cigarettes.

- If she has already started to smoke, set a firm date with her to quit. Then, if she finds she cannot stop, encourage her to talk to former smokers, who will tell her how they managed to quit. If she finds she needs help, she should join an antismoking group or consult a psychiatrist or psychologist who specializes in this area. Her doctor can provide a prescription for slow-release transdermal patches, which contain a small dose of nicotine to help with initial withdrawal symptoms, like headaches, tension or disturbed sleeping patterns. Encourage her to persevere if she values her health and her complexion.

CHAPTER 14

TEENAGE ALCOHOL ABUSE

Binge Drinking

Parents are now facing severe problems caused by heavy alcohol consumption among some adolescents who sneak out of the house for Friday and Saturday night drinking binges. On university campuses and in the social circles of just about any high school teenagers drink to "get wasted" and as a means of having a good time. They ignore the fact that large quantities of alcohol will, over the years, cause stomach ulcers, inflammation and decay of the liver (cirrhosis), liver cancer, heart disease and brain damage. Women, due to their lower body weight, develop these problems far sooner than men do. Alcohol is also the main cause of automobile fatalities in young people.

More Teenage Girls than Boys Drink to Excess

Boys drink more often and have greater body mass, which means they can drink more and have a better knowledge of their own limits. Girls, being somewhat lighter on average, get drunk more quickly and, because they are less likely to be frequent drinkers, do not know their limits so well.

Why Preteen and Teenage Girls Binge Drink

DrugARM, an organization that deals with teenage drug problems, operates throughout Australia and New Zealand. DrugARM's New South Wales director believes low self-esteem and a desire for peer group status are behind most teenage drinking. "Kids out there believe they are immortal," he says sadly. "They fail at school, feel worthless, so they look for something that will give them notoriety and status in their group. If they can't get a good reputation, a bad reputation is better than nothing, far better than being ignored at school or at home. Kids are clever at getting what they want. They steal alcohol from parents or buy it from liquor stores and bars that don't care whom they sell it to."[1]

Some kids ask their parents for money for school lunches; they save up and then get someone of legal age to buy them a case of beer or bottle of liquor. Teenagers can be very resourceful when it comes to purchasing alcohol.

Nationwide, half of all high school students currently drink, with about 30 percent participating in episodic heavy or binge drinking (consumption of five or more drinks in one

---

1. In October 1997, DrugARM's seven vans operating around Sydney helped 1,105 teenagers; staggeringly enough, 90 percent of the kids were found to be drunk (that's a thousand drunk teenagers) according to John O'Hara, who blames the alcohol industry for targeting kids with alcoholic ciders, lemonades and colas.

sitting). Though male students have a somewhat higher rate of alcohol use, by twelfth grade 28 percent of girls admit to binge drinking.

Drinking and Driving

A major problem for young female drinkers is how to get home after an evening's drinking. Some lurch drunkenly across the road and cause traffic accidents. Those injured by cars are carted off by ambulances and end up in the hospital or in the morgue. Others get into cars driven by someone over the legal limit and are involved in a crash.

HOW YOU CAN HELP INFORM YOUR DAUGHTER ABOUT ALCOHOL

- Your daughter should regard alcohol as something to enjoy, but only in moderation. When she turns twelve or thirteen, you may want to let her have a glass of wine (or wine and water, as French children do) with a meal on special occasions, provided she sips and savors it slowly, rather than gulps it. Usually, children who are allowed to sip one glass of wine a night under supervision encounter far fewer problems with alcohol than those banned from "the demon drink," who may then start to drink illegally.
- Explain how drinking liquor or wine, glass after glass, releases inhibitions and can be a crucial factor in unsafe sex. Alcohol takes effect on the brain within ten minutes. Due to lower body weight, most women have a far lower tolerance to alcohol than most men do. Alcoholism causes

liver cancer, heart disease and brain damage, all developed
by women sooner than by men.

■ Tell your daughter never to enter a car when the driver is
under the influence of alcohol or drive herself when she
is over the limit. Ask her to call home if she needs to be
picked up from parties. A cab ride could save her life, as
young partygoers often have little idea of potential dangers after a party.

■ If you discover that your daughter has been binge drinking, ask her the following questions:

• Are you drinking because you have a problem to blot
out or simply to have a good time?

• In a group situation where booze is being passed
around, do you feel calmer when the bottle reaches
you?

• Do you hang on to the bottle longer than your friends
do?

• Are you suffering from short-term memory loss?
For example, can you remember what you wore last
Saturday?

■ If you are worried about your daughter's fondness for alcohol, call your local alcohol and drug information service
for advice; speak to your doctor or local Alcoholics Anonymous chapter.

CHAPTER 15

ILLEGAL DRUGS

Taking or smoking illegal drugs (as well as some legal drugs such as alcohol and tobacco) is seen by many teenagers as an acceptable way to block out problems in our Prozac-taking society. Many kids think that recreational drug use is a good way to enjoy themselves. It is tragic that such a warped message has influenced young people. These are the real facts about illegal drugs:

* There can be absolutely no shortcut to long-lasting happiness by taking or smoking mood-altering drugs: They don't solve anything, and they actually make problems worse.

* Drugs undermine people's physical and mental health, their ambitions and power of thought.

* The effect of drugs wears off quickly so that greater quantities have to be taken to banish "midweek blues" after a weekend's pill popping or injecting.

* Most drugs affect the user's driving skills and coordination, vision and ability to judge distance and speed. Any-

one under the influence of drugs or alcohol who kills or injures another person while driving can be sent to prison. Drugs can be detected by testing blood and urine samples.

Some teenagers refuse to read drug-warning pamphlets; others stop paying attention during school drug-education programs. Drugs are now freely available to the young, often given out as free samples by teenage pushers. Parents *must* read up about drugs and remain one step ahead so they can talk with their children while their kids are still young enough to heed warnings.

Marijuana: The Slow Brain Drain . . . and Worse

Marijuana, pot, cannabis, dope, grass and weed are all names for the dried leaves and the flowers of the hemp plant. Which country has the highest per capita consumption of marijuana? India? Jamaica? The answer is Australia, followed by Holland, where its use was decriminalized decades ago. The Dutch sell it in milk bars and cafes, and masses of teenagers smoke it openly. Illegal consumption in the United States, Britain, most of Europe and New Zealand is considerable.

According to the Substance Abuse and Mental Health Services 1999 National Household Survey on Drug Abuse, 76,428,000 Americans have used marijuana in their lifetime. It is more easily procured than alcohol, so it is widely available in many schools and at parties. Ready-rolled "joints," "reefers," "tokes" or "cones" can be bartered for doing another kid's homework. Schoolkids buy a "joint" and inhale the smoke, curious to know how marijuana will affect them and eager to be part of the "in crowd" that uses it. The majority who experiment with pot do not become regular users, but some will.

Passing around "joints" means saliva is passed on as well, with the consequence that smokers with ulcers or tiny cuts in their mouth can catch hepatitis. Some who smoke pot inhale amyl nitrate or "rush" at the same time to achieve a bigger high.

A small minority "snow cone" (adding cocaine to their "cone"). Relative to pot, cocaine is expensive, so its use is low among the young. Apart from "snow coning" cocaine can be snorted or injected, like heroin, making the user feel confident and relaxed.

What Makes Today's Marijuana More Toxic?

Cannabis is the equivalent of Prozac for today's teenagers and far more widely available. The chemical in cannabis, which gives users a high, is tetrahydrocannabinol (THC). THC affects the mood as well as perceptions of the user. It reduces will power and, taken over an extended period, causes short-term memory loss. Hashish is a much stronger form, manufactured by compressing marijuana resins into small blocks. It can be mixed with tobacco and then smoked. Hash is extremely potent. Those who have used hash discover that the THC level in it is so highly concentrated that even a small amount will produce a high. Marijuana or hash marinated in butter or oil can be put into a brownie mix, baked and served as "pot brownies."

This mind-altering drug contains 421 known chemicals, some of which remain stored in body fat and in the brain for up to one month before being excreted from the body. Some of these chemicals and the tar content of marijuana are as harmful to lungs when inhaled, even in small quantities, as those in tobacco. The real problem (which some people choose to ignore) stems from the fact that users of marijuana are now smoking "improved" or hybrid strains, like sensimilla, which contain at least 15 percent THC and are far stronger than the strains hippies smoked back in the 1960s, when marijuana contained only 3 percent THC. In the 1960s, pot smokers would have needed a "joint" as long as an axe handle to inhale the same quantity of THC as present in one single "joint" today! Harmful effects of heavy pot smoking are loss of short-term memory and concentration, lack of all will power and motivation, detachment from reality and anxiety. Loss of concentration is what makes it hard for heavy marijuana smokers to achieve good grades at school or hold down a responsible job. Pushers don't explain that what they are selling as "high-quality" pot, guaranteed to give a really big high, may be "cut" with cocaine or heroin. This can lead to addiction of the buyer (and profit for dealers).

Many girls experiment with pot. Some will decide they don't like it; others smoke a few "joints" but will eventually give it up. A third and smaller group will smoke heavily. Unfortunately for pot smokers, home-rolled "joints" lack filter tips, and "bongs" (a plastic water bottle with a hose attached) do not filter out tar. Hardened pot smokers inhale deeply and delay exhaling, which can eventually cause lung cancer, because sticky tar builds up in their lungs.

Manufactured or "Designer" Drugs

Figures for experimentation with designer drugs are higher than ever before. Most designer drugs (as well as heroin and cocaine) are sold at all-night parties ("raves") held in night-clubs, empty houses or abandoned warehouses, which are advertised in video stores or on the Internet. All over the world, many thousands of teenagers put themselves into a trancelike state after popping pills or powders.

Teenagers often mix a cocktail of designer drugs, alcohol and tranquilizers, trying to avoid the depression that follows drug taking and those "midweek blues" that play havoc with school study. Taking a drug cocktail often makes users vomit and can cause "road rage," violence, bouts of paranoia or even death.

Users become hooked on the highs and return to week-end raves for a further dose. Point out to your daughter that tablets manufactured in illegal laboratories carry *no* guarantee. Buyers cannot tell which tablets are lethal and which are not. Teenage and adult pushers who sell kids the tablets are certainly not going to issue health warnings.

Amphetamines (Speed, Whiz or Uppers)

Due to their cheapness, these are now the second most popular recreational drugs for kids after marijuana. Made in back-street laboratories or houses rented for this purpose, amphetamines lack quality control and are often bulked out with substances like talcum, glucose, lactose or caffeine.

The tablets are offered through a distribution chain *by* kids *to* kids. Over the past decade, party drug use has more than doubled among the fourteen to twenty-four age group, many of whom see nothing wrong in taking them. The artificially induced euphoria lasts only a few hours. The drug makes the user's brain produce more dopamine, which initially creates a sense of energy and well-being. Some teenagers claim speed intensifies the music at discos and parties and gives them confidence.

Initially amphetamines were sold legally to keep soldiers and pilots awake during World War II. Later they were sold by chemists as an antiasthma drug, to keep drivers or students awake or to suppress appetite among the overweight (girls still buy illegal amphetamines for weight control, although their effect on blood pressure can be dangerous). Harmful side effects caused amphetamines to be withdrawn from the market in the 1970s. Drug pushers started distributing them illegally and made huge sums.

In tablet, capsule or powder form, speed can be swallowed, injected with needles, smoked, drunk in alcohol or fruit juice or "snorted" like cocaine. The color varies from white, cream or yellow to brown. Liquid speed is deep red. Schoolchildren are advised by the pushers that taking speed will help them stay awake when studying for exams or attending all-night parties. No one mentions the low that follows. The vaunted high or "buzz" of happiness generally lasts between three and four hours. Side effects can include some (but not all) of the following:

* Brief periods of self-confidence, invincibility and the illusion of happiness or high followed by a corresponding low

that will affect schoolwork or any form of part-time job
- Sweating, irregular heartbeat and nosebleeds from "snorting"
- Lack of concentration and appetite, restlessness, dizziness, fever, fainting and mild paranoia
- Sudden mood swings, violent acts and unconsciousness
- Long-term damage including amphetamine psychosis, anxiety attacks, clinical depression, suicidal thoughts and (through shared needles) exposure to AIDS or hepatitis B infection, which can be fatal

LSD and Ecstasy

These drugs interfere with the brain's ability to store experience. They overload the cortex with sensory input, causing visions where colors split and explode and even a mundane object seems to promise infinity. Due to its high cost, Ecstasy has now become less popular than amphetamines.

Ecstasy was developed as an appetite suppressant, then used by psychiatrists in the United States in combination with LSD to release patients' inhibitions until, after a series of disasters, it was banned as being far too dangerous to use. Later, backyard laboratories in Britain, Europe and Australia started manufacturing Ecstasy illegally, using talcum powder as a filler and setting prices ranging from forty to sixty dollars per tablet. Then some dealers started selling much cheaper but fake "E" tablets. These were nothing more than dog-worming pills or those large white toxic tablets bought cheaply from aquarium shops to control gill fluke and fish lice. These fish tablets cost their pushers only about a dollar each and gave their users a quick "buzz" or high before causing vomiting.

Genuine Ecstasy tablets vary in color depending which illegal laboratory made them. They can be white, cream, pink, yellow or green, sometimes with brown flecks, depending on what fillers bulk them out, or they can be sold in powder form. "Ekkies," "E" or "White Doves" and speed keep users awake so they can dance all night.

LSD "trips" look like small pieces of blotting paper. LSD is cheaper than Ecstasy and makes users feel alert, confident and energetic. At high doses users can become paranoid and, after some hours, many vomit. In large quantities, it has unpredictable side effects, and used in combination with marijuana it can be dangerous. LSD users have been known to jump out of multistory buildings, laughing as they went. All over the world, ageing patients with LSD-induced schizophrenia are frittering away their lives in psychiatric wards or halfway houses, thanks to this drug.

Ketamine ("Special K")

Ketamine is an animal anaesthetic with hallucinogenic properties similar to LSD. It has also become a party drug. In high doses, ketamine can cause users to lose consciousness.

Benzodiazepine (Rohypnol, "Roofies" or "Date Rape" Tablets)

Unsuspecting girls and women have had benzodiazepine added to their drinks and have been "assisted" from nightclubs and parties by "friendly" men who then raped them. Rohypnol can be fatal when mixed with heroin.

Gamma Hydroxy Butyrate ("Fantasy," "Grievous Bodily Harm" or "GHB")

This is a clear liquid sold in small glass bottles. Mixed with alcohol it can put users into intensive care wards on respirators and has caused several deaths. "Blue Nitro" is another horrible "cocktail" mix of GHB derivative with heroin and amphetamines.

Methylamphetamine ("Shabu," "Superspeed" or "Super-Amphetamine")

The latest research suggests that methylamphetamine is rising in popularity due to its low price. Like speed and Ecstasy it is manufactured in illegal laboratories and has caused hundreds of deaths. At two to four dollars a tablet, "shabu" is far cheaper and more deadly than crack cocaine or heroin and is highly addictive. Shabu tablets resemble Ecstasy but are cheaper and far more dangerous. The Australian Drug Law Reform Foundation warns that "shabu" and amphetamines appear to be set to take over as the most widely used recreational drugs. Blue Star tattoos are also very new and sold to kids. These self-adhesive tattoos contain a percentage of amphetamine or super-amphetamine that is slowly released into the blood stream.

Ecstasy and Anna Wood

Anna Wood was outgoing, popular and part of an affectionate group of friends who adored her. Her parents were united, stable and loving. Anna had everything to live for. She was pretty, had a bubbly personality, had a happy home life and was about to leave school and take her "dream job" as a beautician.

Like many fifteen-year-olds, Anna was eager to attend a Saturday night "rave" in the city, but, fearing her parents would forbid it, she told a white lie. She reassured her parents she was only going to watch videos at her friend Chloe's house and sleep over there.

Unknown to her parents, Anna and her group of friends aimed to attend a "rave," take Ecstasy and have a good time.

Each girl paid sixty dollars for an "E" tablet. Anna bought her lethal tablet from Samantha X, a senior at Anna's high school. Samantha had been dealing for some time and stood outside the entrance to the all-night "rave" selling Ecstasy. Anna had been against heroin and other hard drugs but had occasionally smoked marijuana and had once taken half an Ecstasy tablet. Some of her friends had experimented with a range of drugs, although Anna had told them they were stupid to do so. On this particular occasion, Anna bought and swallowed with water a whole "E" tablet, worried that taking half, like her friends, might not give her "a good trip." Anna danced for hours, saying, "This is the best night of my life."

She became very thirsty. As Anna didn't want to drink alcohol, she drank masses of water. She danced on . . . and on . . . and on.

At five o'clock in the morning, Anna started vomiting. Rave-goers are used to this, as it happens a great deal to kids on Ecstasy or a cocktail of drugs. However, Anna's vomiting continued for so long that her friends became alarmed. By now her eyes were rolling wildly, and she had no idea where she was. Her friends dragged her into a car and drove to her friend Chloe's home, where Anna continued vomiting and lost consciousness.

Anna's mother, Angela Wood, was called. She summoned an ambulance, which sped her to the hospital. Terrified of the police, Anna's friends lied to cover up the fact that they had all taken "E."

They told the ambulance driver that Anna's drink had been "spiked." Finally, at the hospital, Anna's terrified friends confessed they had all taken Ecstasy. By now it was too late. Doctors ordered a cerebral angiogram, which showed that Anna's brain had swollen with all the water she had drunk, so no blood or oxygen could reach it. She was brain dead.

Anna's friends and family were confused, angry and distraught by her death. They demanded to know how a fellow pupil at Anna's school could sell a trusting young girl with her whole life ahead of her a tablet that would kill her.

The police took the matter very seriously. Samantha, the girl who had sold Anna the fatal "E" tablet, was arrested, tried and found guilty. Samantha and her family employed a top lawyer, who made emotional pleas about her youth as an extenuating factor, and she got off relatively lightly.

Angela Wood has converted her grief and anger over her daughter's death into a crusade to save other teenagers. An excellent speaker, Angela visits schools and parent groups, lecturing on the dangers of drug abuse. "I see speaking in public as the gift Anna left me, to save other kids from what happened to her," Angela says.

HOW YOU CAN HELP INFORM YOUR
DAUGHTER ABOUT DRUGS

■ The time to talk with your daughter about drugs is *before* she and her friends start using them. Under the age of ten, most kids still listen to *your* beliefs and *your* advice. This is when you should warn her about the bad long-term effects of drugs.

■ Warn your toddler not to taste anything she finds on the ground or in packets either on the streets or in parks. Explain that it could be a substance that could harm her or make her sick.

■ Explain the difference between "good" medical drugs and bad or illegal drugs when she is six or seven. If your daughter gets sick and is prescribed a "good" drug, use this as an opportunity to explain how important it is not to overuse medication or turn to "bad" drugs when she is older.

■ Between nine and eleven, your daughter will slowly start to move away from your influence. If, at this age, you haven't informed her about the dangers of drugs, she will hear about them from friends or through the mass media, possibly in a distorted way.

■ Don't leave drug education entirely to her school. Talk with your teenager about what drug education she is getting. Do not give her a lecture. A drive or a shopping expedition can be a good place for a quiet chat. Ask nonchalantly how many girls in her class smoke pot or take recreational drugs. Her answer could surprise you. Remember, many "nice," intelligent kids now buy and experiment with a cocktail of drugs, some with fatal results.

■ Let your daughter know that, although tripping on LSD provides beautiful floating feelings, it can also give "bad trips," and under its influence people have killed themselves in car accidents or through suicide. LSD (and/or contaminated heroin) is often added to "E" tablets, LSD being far cheaper to manufacture than Ecstasy.

■ Warn your daughter against getting into a car with anyone who has taken drugs of any kind, as that person's judgment will be seriously impaired.

■ Get all the information you can to help your daughter resist sales pressure from the kids who now push drugs in many schools. Some kids offer trial "hits" for free. Discuss with your daughter exactly why they do this: Is it because they like her, or do they do it to build up their sales and make more money?

HOW YOU CAN HELP IF YOUR DAUGHTER IS ON DRUGS

■ Should you find what you think is pot or a bong (plastic bottle with a piece of hose attached) in your daughter's room, you should not blame yourself for bad parenting. Many "good" parents are struggling with their children's drug abuse today. Making an angry scene doesn't help. Don't stop parenting at this point. Ask if she takes drugs to have fun or to escape from reality. Recommend counseling, and go with her initially. If possible, she shouldn't come home to an empty house. Be there for her, even if she doesn't want to talk about drugs or any other problem. Be consistent, and remember that teenagers *need* an adult authority figure to react against, which should be you!

■ If your daughter comes home from a party high on drugs, don't try to discuss anything until the next day. Stay calm; anger won't help you or her. Look in your phone book, contact your local community drug and alcohol service (you don't need to give your name) or other voluntary antidrug organizations who are discreet and experienced. If in doubt, ask your family doctor to recommend one, and find a counselor whose approach suits you.

■ Don't give your daughter a large allowance that could be a temptation to buy more drugs.

■ Always check up with other children's parents if your daughter asks to stay overnight with a friend.

■ Join a parents' group run by an antidrug organization with whom you feel in sympathy. At this difficult time you and your partner need support and practical help. Group support works well for parents driven to despair; trying to live with an adolescent on drugs causes trauma in everyone's lives.

■ If your daughter brings drugs home, you have the right to insist that your house remains drug-free and/or call the police if you fear younger siblings may start taking drugs. If your daughter is under eighteen, she may appear in juvenile or criminal court, depending on a long list of criteria. Each case is different, and each family reacts differently. By now you may need a social worker, counselor or psychiatrist specializing in this area to provide help.

■ Tell your daughter that no one on "E" should drink alcohol or take more than 17 ounces of water while dancing or 8.5 ounces while sitting down. Alcohol, if combined with

Ecstasy, liquid "E," Ketamine or Fantasy, can cause kidney or brain failure.

■ If your teenager goes to raves regularly, make sure she can recognize symptoms of drug overdose, such as nausea and vomiting, fainting, inability to urinate, overheating or convulsions.

■ If your daughter attends raves tell her that if someone who has taken "E" vomits or faints an ambulance *must* be called. Meanwhile, someone should fan the sufferer to keep his or her body temperature down. When the ambulance arrives, the driver *must* be told exactly what the person has taken. Doctors need to know what drugs have been taken to treat a drug patient successfully.

■ If teenagers throw a party in your house, make certain you stay home, however unpopular it makes you with your kids. Say firmly to any young guest who smokes pot, "You are welcome to do whatever you like in your own home. But, as a guest in my house, please respect my way of life." Parents have rights. Insist that party-crashers leave immediately. Gate-crashers could bring with them "spiked" alcohol or illegal drugs, with dire consequences for you and your children.

CHAPTER 16

VIOLENCE AGAINST YOUR DAUGHTER

That your child might suffer the pain and humiliation of childhood sexual abuse or of rape or sexual assault as a teenager seems unthinkable. But it happens often enough that parents should think about how to respond if it happens to their daughter.

Childhood Sexual Assault and Incest

Today, according to Centers of Disease Control statistics, 22.1 percent of girls younger than fifteen have been forcefully introduced to sexual intercourse. In spite of media hype about wicked strangers and organized pedophilia, most perpetrators are known to the child and are very often in a relationship of trust—father, stepfather, grandfather, uncle or longtime family friend. This dreadful betrayal of trust adds a great psychological burden to the physical harm inflicted on the child.

It is, of course, a betrayal of the mother's trust, too. It may be very hard to believe that this can happen, because it involves not only accepting that your daughter has been violated and hurt but that someone you love and trust has done this. Yet your daughter's capacity to cope will be affected by your ability to acknowledge what has happened and to respond to it.

Other things can also confuse a mother's reaction. There is sometimes an unwillingness to face the facts of incest and sexual abuse in our society, and sometimes attempts are made to downplay it. Some people, even some in responsible professional positions, think children make up this sort of thing. Perhaps a few do, but fantasy like this could indicate that something is wrong somewhere; a wise parent would consider what this might be rather than ignore it.

Children expect that adults, especially those close to them, will protect them from pain and harm. When, instead, they inflict this upon a child, she is betrayed, confused and may feel somehow guilty and responsible. It can be hard to trust anyone afterward.

This makes it very difficult to tell another loved authority figure, even a mother, about the abuse, particularly as the child is sworn to secrecy or threatened. She may feel "dirty" and ashamed and think she has somehow forfeited the right to receive help. She will realize that her mother will find it incredible that someone she knows, a friend or relation, could do this. Very few children disclose sexual abuse. Therefore, if your daughter has enough courage and faith in you to tell you, directly or indirectly, that she has been subjected to unwanted sexual activity, she deserves your wholehearted support.

You and your daughter may both need help to come to terms with the situation: medical or psychological attention and advice about what to do next and how to minimize possible long-term effects. Contact your doctor, one of the specialized organizations listed in the telephone directory, or call the National Child Abuse Hotline at 1-800-4-A-CHILD. They will not be shocked—sadly, they will have heard many stories like yours before. Childhood sexual abuse is most commonly inflicted on girls by men, so your daughter may be more comfortable if the people you ask to help her are women, particularly when it comes to any physical examination.

Although childhood sexual abuse is a criminal offence, the process of bringing the perpetrator to justice can be long and very painful. It can be hard to get a conviction, and if the victim knows the offender walked out of the court unconvicted, this would be the final betrayal and sign that she is of little value in our society. You might think that taking the matter to the law would do more harm than good. Talk it over with someone you trust, bearing in mind that there are matters that professionals working with children may, by law, have to report to the police.

It may be a good idea to talk to her teacher so together you can work out ways to ensure her education doesn't suffer. Love, reassurance and acceptance at home will be of fundamental importance. Obviously, protection from situations where she could be vulnerable to further abuse is essential.

What happened to your daughter and the blow to her self-esteem and ability to trust others may lead to a number of problems, ranging from poor concentration at school and isolation from friends to high-risk behavior during the turbulent teenage years and difficulties in personal and sexual relationships as an adult.

High-risk behavior can include smoking, drinking or bingeing alcohol or using illegal drugs. It may take the form of promiscuity or not using contraceptives and condoms to protect against pregnancy and sexually transmitted infections. Studies show that a high proportion of young teenage mothers have suffered childhood sexual abuse. The reasons for this are complex, but low self-esteem and feeling that sex is the way to approval are likely to be factors.

Pregnancy and labor can be more difficult for women of any age who have been victims of violence. These women often face more health problems than other mothers, and their babies are likely to weigh less at birth, which can mean more health risks for them.

No matter how old your daughter is when she becomes pregnant, intimate physical examinations and labor can trigger or revive memories of the past abuse. This can cause reactions that neither she nor her midwife or doctor understand and can affect the care she receives. Suggest that things will be better for her and the baby if she tells her main caregiver about the abuse. At this time she may be more comfortable being looked after by women rather than by male doctors or nurses.

Rape and Sexual Assault

What can you do if the unthinkable happens and your daughter is raped or sexually assaulted? Rape crisis centers now exist in all big cities, and there are also free anonymous telephone crisis lines. Look them up (they are usually listed in the front of the telephone directory) and suggest to your daughter that you or she contact a center. One national hot line, the Rape Abuse and Incest National Network, is provided by the Family Crisis Center and can be reached twenty-four hours a day at 800-656-HOPE (4673). Emergency services offer help and counseling or refer you to other services if necessary. They are staffed by specially trained women who usually have a very woman-centered outlook on the world.

These specialized services are not just for help at the time of the incident. Your daughter could find them useful even if the rape or assault happened a while ago. Even if she has rejected these services before, remind her about them as time passes in case she changes her mind or needs more support as she works through what has happened.

Get appropriate medical help. The emergency departments of most hospitals have guidelines to make sure victims of violence are seen quickly and treated sensitively. You may prefer to go to your general practitioner, especially if she has a good rapport with your daughter. Rape or sexual assault may or may not involve immediate physical injury. Research suggests that it can also cause long-term health problems. In addition to making sure your daughter gets medical attention in relation to possible injury, infections or pregnancy, you need to know of the chance of long-term effects on her health.

Always respect your daughter's decisions. What happened to her took away her dignity and autonomy, her control over her body and most intimate aspects of her life. This feeling of powerlessness could have a more lasting impact on her than any physical injuries. It is very important not to reinforce the feeling of helplessness by making decisions for her or by over-looking her opinions and feelings about what should happen next. This may be very difficult in an acute crisis, but at least make sure she understands that you are trying to support and help her until she can take control again herself.

This is no time for recriminations. Bite back any criticism that may come to you in your anger, denial or distress. Remember, no girl ever deserves to be raped or sexually assaulted. Victims are never responsible for the violence inflicted upon them—no one has any right or excuse to treat another person in a way that degrades and hurts her like this.

Recognize that the violation of your daughter can be a trauma, though of a different kind, for you. Don't be afraid to ask for help for yourself. You will be able to support your daughter better if you are coping better yourself.

Report the matter to the police if your daughter agrees to this. Obviously, you should contact the police as soon as pos-sible if you want to file criminal charges. Your daughter should understand that she will have to undergo physical examina-tion and answer a lot of questions that would be unpleasant and embarrassing at the best of times. She will probably have to tell several people what has happened, in a way repeating and reliving the event.

These days there are more women among the doctors who do the forensic examinations. And, like the police who deal with cases of sexual violence, they usually have special train-ing to enable them to satisfy all the legal requirements as sen-sitively as possible. You, or someone else your daughter would like to support her, can be with her. The rape crisis centers can usually provide an experienced woman to do this if she would be more comfortable that way.

Most victims don't report rape unless it was inflicted by a stranger or they were physically injured. Charges are not always brought against the perpetrator if they do report it. Many find the idea of going through the experience again in front of a court just too much. Again, the decision must be your daughter's, with calm advice from you and other members of the family and maybe your own doctor or lawyer if you have one. Obviously, this advice must look to your daughter's best interests and long-term healing, though it may sometimes be hard to overcome gut reactions for vengeance.

HOW YOU CAN HELP IF YOUR DAUGHTER IS SEXUALLY ASSAULTED

- Listen to your daughter. Recognize that you may instinctively want to deny what she is trying to tell you or to avoid dealing with it. Remember, it is even harder for her to tell you about it than it is for you to hear about it.
- Believe your daughter when she has the trust and courage to tell you what happened. If you deny her this acknowledgment, you reinforce her sense of betrayal and alienation.
- Trust her. Don't recriminate or put your feelings or family interests before hers. She is your daughter and has a right to your support and protection.
- Encourage and support her to regain control. As a victim of sexual assault she has had her autonomy and control over her body torn from her. She needs you to help her

make decisions about what to do next, not to make them for her.

■ Seek professional help with her consultation and agreement.

■ Make sure she knows you love her, accept her and support her in this crisis and whatever may follow. Reassure her often that the victim is not the guilty party and that while she may feel ashamed about what happened, she was not to blame.

Domestic Violence

If you are in a situation of domestic violence, your children are likely to be harmed by it. This may be through physical injury, though the psychological and emotional impact of living in a violent household can have an effect as profound as actual physical violence. Children are almost always aware of violence in their home and very often experience it themselves. Inevitably, their own distress is made worse by knowing about their parent's suffering.

It is easy for outsiders to give glib advice about leaving a violent relationship and taking children to a safer environment. Only you can decide what you can or should do. Investigate your options. The National Domestic Violence Hotline can help provide emotional support and refer you to specialized services that help women in this situation in your area. The hotline can be reached at 800-799-SAFE (7233) and can provide contacts for information and referral centers and

> **You and your children must remember that those who behave violently toward others are responsible for their actions. No one else is.**

refuges and safe places where you and your children can stay until you decide what to do next.

Think long and hard about the accepted wisdom that a stable home with both parents is best for children, no matter what it is like. You can discuss this with your daughter if she is old enough, bearing in mind that, like you, she is probably confused and ambivalent, torn between her love for her other parent and the horror and fear of what he sometimes does. She may blame you, or herself. She needs to know that violence is never justified, never an acceptable response, no matter what provokes it.

The decision to leave a violent relationship is a very difficult one, unless you or the children are obviously at great immediate risk. If you decide to reject your situation as unsafe for you and your children, discuss your choice with your daughter. If you don't, she may misunderstand and blame you for separating her from her other parent. The role of the single parent is not easy, but you will cope better if both of you understand why this seemed the best option.

It is not uncommon for children to feel somehow responsible for the violence inflicted by one parent on the other. They are not, and every effort should be made to let them know this.

CHAPTER 17

SEXUALLY TRANSMITTED DISEASES

According to general practitioner Dr. Jean Sparling, there is evidence to show that those girls who receive the most information are the least likely to develop dangerous sexual habits. Dr. Sparling is known by her patients as an excellent communicator. She explains the importance of getting your pubescent daughter to come to terms with the danger of sexually transmitted diseases (STDs), which can seriously affect her health and jeopardize her future.

Normal Vaginal Health

The healthy vagina contains moisture in the form of mucus coming from the gland in the neck of the womb (cervix); this gland manufactures a small amount of clear vaginal discharge with a characteristic "female" smell, which will normally leave a yellow color on the underpants. The vagina always contains organisms, bacteria, fungi and viruses, which are a normal part of the contents and form a well-functioning and healthy ecosystem. The normal vagina does not need cleaning with douches, creams or perfumed sprays. Contrary to the advertising for them, these will only upset nature's perfectly balanced system. If your daughter has any vaginal discharge in excess of the normal, any itching or offensive odor whatsoever, she should see a doctor.

The infections described on the following pages are roughly in order of frequency rather than their danger to health and well-being.

Chlamydia

Chlamydia is the most common bacterial STD in the United States with an estimated three million new cases every year. Chlamydia normally has an incubation period of one to two weeks, but it may be slightly longer. Often the infection causes no obvious symptoms. When there are symptoms, these consist of a vaginal discharge (watery or sticky), itching and pain on passing urine. The most likely person to suffer from chlamydia infection is a sexually active female under twenty-five who is in a monogamous relationship and whose partner is not using condoms. The disease often occurs when the girl changes partners. The main complication of the disease is its spread to the pelvic area with an infection in the womb and fallopian tubes (the tubes through which the eggs from the ovaries travel to enter into the womb) which, in many cases, can lead to infertility.

Diagnosis is usually made from laboratory testing of urine or from a swab taken, possibly when having a pap smear.

Urine samples are more reliable, as they do not need the organism to be kept alive for testing.

Treatment

One oral dose of azithromycin will eradicate this organism. It is important to trace all sexual contacts the girl may have had, going back for several months if possible.

Candidiasis or Yeast Infection

Candidiasis is an infection caused by the fungus candida and may or may not be a result of intercourse. It can be acquired through sexual contact or in a wide variety of other ways, including taking broad-spectrum antibiotics (an unwelcome side effect of which may be the killing of "good" protective vaginal flora, thus causing candida to flourish), wearing tight nylon pants or sitting around for long periods in a damp bathing suit. Candida is often found in chronic invalids or following a debilitating illness.

Candida presents as a very itchy, white, cheesy vaginal discharge without an odor. It causes intense discomfort. It often mimics the feeling of sexual arousal but then makes sexual intercourse disagreeable or even painful for the female partner, though not for the male.

Treatment

One of several antifungal agents may be applied by vaginal applicator. Tablets are also given by mouth, as the candida may have lodged in the bowel. It is important that the girl's partner is also treated with antifungals, because he may well have been infected with candida. Even though the male appears to have no symptoms, he may still be able to pass candida on (or "ping-pong" the candida back again) by having sex with a girl who is undergoing antifungal treatment.[1]

Genital Herpes

The herpes simplex virus infects most people as cold sores, eye infections or genital herpes at some time in their lives. In the United States, about one in five people over the age of twelve, about forty-five million individuals, are infected with the virus that causes genital herpes. Though a sexually transmitted disease with a relatively high incidence rate, genital or herpes simplex virus type II no longer spells disaster to any young woman's sex life. The incubation period varies from three to six days. At first the infected area feels hypersensitive; this is soon followed by a group of small painful ulcers on the labia, on the clitoris or inside the vagina. There may be similar lesions in the mouth and throat following oral sex. These symptoms may persist for up to three weeks. In those who have not previously met the virus in any form, initial infection may be extremely painful and debilitating (rendering vaginal sex out of the question both from the aspect of pain and from the danger of infecting a partner). A swab taken from the ulcer is the most effective way of making a diagnosis.

Treatment

Antiviral agents such as acyclovir and valaciclovir are prescribed. It is most important to treat the initial illness promptly and properly. Improperly treated genital herpes is a relapsing condition, occurring over many years, that has profound sexual and social consequences. It is important to realize that this condition may be transmitted even when no ulcers are visible. A cure is seldom achieved. Repeated courses or continuous treatment may be required to keep the patient symptom-free. Relapse may be associated with physical or emotional stress, fever, menstruation and many other conditions affecting well-being.

Genital Warts

Human papilloma virus (HPV), also known as venereal or genital warts, is usually sexually acquired, and an estimated twenty million people in the United States are currently infected, with 5.5 million new infections projected annually. These warts, sometimes but not always painful, usually occur around the openings to the vagina or bowel. Lesions may occur up to six months after infection. The wart virus can be a cause of cancer of the neck of the womb. Warts may be small and flat on cool dry areas or large and feathery on moist areas. Warts on the neck of the womb often have no symptoms. As they are not visible, they remain undetected and are usually found coincidentally when a lab is checking on the patient's pap smear. Many different types of wart virus have been identified. Some viruses have a low risk of cervical cancer, while others are associated with a markedly higher risk. Factors such as smoking, numbers of sexual partners, lowered immunity and the presence of other sexually transmissible infections also influence the development of HPV-induced cervical cancer.

Treatment

External warts are treated with local application of podophyl-
lotoxin gel. This is best done either by your doctor or a family
member. It is not recommended that girls treat themselves. If
this treatment is not successful or the warts are internal, other
methods, such as cryotherapy and laser treatment, are available through your doctor. Patients with genital warts must be
checked for other STDs. In view of the risk of cancer, it is
most important to have regular follow-up pap smear tests.
There is a high recurrence rate, even after treatment. HPV
vaccines are currently being developed, and future patient
management may well be by this means.

HIV-AIDS

Acquired Immunodeficiency Syndrome (AIDS) follows infection with Human Immunodeficiency Virus (HIV), acquired
through exchange of infected semen, saliva or blood. Worldwide, an estimated 36.1 million people are living with AIDS.
As of June 2001, 422,086 individuals in the United States
were living with AIDS or HIV, according to the Centers for
Disease Control.

Clinically, this is an acute illness with fever, night sweats,
malaise and acute discomfort, headache, general aches and
pains and a generalized rash that occurs about six weeks after
the initial infection. Chronic lethargy and depression may persist long after the acute phase of the illness has passed. Blood
tests usually become positive within the first three months following infection. After this, most people enter a phase where
they are symptom-free, which lasts for a period ranging from
several months to many years. However, HIV-AIDS is a com-

plex disease and can have many variations. Since it was first diagnosed, there have been major advances in our knowledge of HIV infection. There are follow-up tests to assess the progress of this disease, and several new drugs are now available to slow its progress.

Treatment

Treatment currently consists of a combination of drugs, which have been found to work much better than any one drug used alone. A lone drug is disadvantaged by the ease with which the virus can develop resistance to it. Combination therapy reduces this factor. The aim of treatment is to keep the patient as well as possible for as long as possible. At present there is no known cure for this fatal disease, although some people remain well for prolonged periods.

Hepatitis B

Hepatitis B is a serious viral infection, causing permanent damage to the liver and, in some cases, death. It is transmitted in exactly the same ways as AIDS but is even more infectious. Hepatitis B is often ignored next to AIDS, though the prevalence and incidence rates are comparable. In the United States, an estimated 77,000 new cases of sexually transmitted hepatitis B occur yearly, and about 750,000 individuals are living with the infection.

Treatment

There is no really effective treatment once the disease is caught. Fortunately, there is now a vaccine to prevent it, and this vaccine can be given to a child along with his or her other shots. Vaccination is to be given to eleven- and twelve-year-olds with two injections, one month apart, and a booster dose after six months. Side effects are minimal, and vaccination is strongly advised.

Trichomoniasis

Trichomoniasis (pronounced trick-oh-moan-eye-aysis) is a common cause of vaginal infection. Sexual intercourse is the principal means of transmission. The incubation period varies from four days to four weeks after sexual contact. It presents as a vaginal discharge that is foul-smelling, frothy, yellow-green and purulent. Some patients also have an intense vulval itch or tenderness, making intercourse unpleasant. Others have no symptoms at all from this disease. Diagnosis is made in the laboratory from a vaginal swab of the discharge taken by the doctor.

Treatment
Specific antibiotics are taken by mouth. Sexual partner(s) should be notified.

Gonorrhea

Though not fatal, gonorrhea can have serious complications if not properly treated. Approximately 650,000 cases of gonorrhea occur annually in the United States, and in about 10 to 40 percent of cases, the infection may ascend to the upper pelvis and result in infection of the womb and fallopian tubes, resulting in permanent infertility.

Gonorrhea has an incubation period of two to seven days but may vary from twenty-four hours to a month. The disease often goes unnoticed because there may be no symptoms at all. If symptoms do occur, these can include vaginal discharge, frequent urination, painful intercourse, malaise, aching, fever and abdominal and joint pain. Some women have a heavy, yellowish vaginal discharge accompanied by irritation. Diagnosis is made by a swab taken from the vagina.

Treatment

Antibiotics usually bring a cure.

Syphilis

Previously thought to be well under control, syphilis is now on the increase again in certain parts of the world and in certain communities. Incubation is about twenty-one days after contact. The first manifestation is the chancre, a firm, painless, punched-out ulcer on the vulva or inside it. If this chancre goes unnoticed, it will get better on its own. The glands in the groin are usually enlarged, firm but not painful. Untreated, the disease persists in the body for as long as twenty years in some cases, ending in insanity and eventual death. If the chancre is detected (and this is rare), material taken from the base of the lesion may reveal the organism. Blood tests are also helpful.

Treatment

Treatment is by antibiotics, and, unlike during the grim days of World War I, when syphilis swept through the population and killed many, it is now curable.

Scabies

Scabies is a form of dermatitis that is not usually regarded as an STD but can be acquired by sleeping with someone with scabies or being in close contact for a prolonged period. Following infestation by the mite *Sarcoptes scabiei*, a month or so later nocturnal itching and a rash will appear on hands, wrists, forearms, waist, inner thighs, buttocks and ankles. The mites, which burrow into the skin, can be seen under magnification.

Treatment

Creams such as benzyl benzoate or lindane 1 percent cream are applied. Bed linen and clothing should be treated.

HOW YOU CAN HELP PREVENT YOUR DAUGHTER FROM CONTRACTING STDS

- Tell your daughter to always insist on "no condom, no sex," as the pill provides no protection whatsoever against STDs. Due to the dangers of oral infection with hepatitis B and AIDS, oral condoms are now available.
- Teach your daughter to respect her own body. Accurate information about bodily changes, STDs, vaginal infections and the good and bad points of condoms are essential to help her understand the vital importance of safe sex practices. If you provide answers to her questions from an early age, there is no embarrassment because to her this is "just another part of learning" and has no different connotation from learning how to cross the street. When she is young is the time to communicate your own sexual and family values. Show her what loyalty, trust and other val-

ues important to you mean and how they work. Teaching by example works far better than "preaching."

■ Give her the facts while she is still young enough to listen, rather than in the phase when she will not wish to be questioned by an anxious parent and will go to great lengths to avoid this. Explain before puberty to your daughter that the emphasis on safety for women has now changed from the need to avoid pregnancy to the very real dangers of STDs. Explain that safe sex includes measures she must take in order to prevent unwanted pregnancy, minimize the chances of contracting a sexually transmitted infection and avoid the violence associated with sexual activity, prevalent today.

■ Remind your daughter that there is no truth to the myth that the contraceptive pill provides them with protection from STDs—in reality it only lessens the risk of pregnancy. The pill has absolutely no effect on lessening the dangers of diseases acquired by sexual means. Many infections can now be transmitted through sexual activity. Some are insignificant; others can be deadly. You and your daughter must learn about them, so that she can be alerted to the dangers, avoid them if possible, and, if not, at least be aware of warning signs.

IN CONCLUSION

It is exciting to learn that more and more girls are attending medical school and have a growing representation in traditionally male university departments such as science, architecture and engineering. A century ago girls were often refused admittance to anything but the university arts faculties. Although we must be aware of the perils girls face today, we should also celebrate their successes.

Most of the contributors to this book worked outside the home when they had young children, so they know the hard realities working parents face in raising a family. They are aware of the fact that there is no substitute for parents spending time with their children.

Some of the sections were distressing to compile. However, parents must be well informed so they can protect their daughters in a world where teenage sex, recreational drug taking and binge drinking are seen on television as well as in real life. Parents must be fully aware of the fact that risk-taking behavior can easily place their daughters in serious danger. The old proverb remains true today: "Parents should trust their kids but keep their eyes wide open."

The recent trend of glorification of on-screen violence gives a distorted impression of reality to children, many of whom have difficulty in distinguishing between fact and fantasy. In some cases, this can lead to "copycat" crime; recent school massacres have caused increased concern over the effect of violence shown on television. News footage of victims of wars, ethnic cleansing and earthquakes can be desensitizing or disturbing. Young children who are upset by such images need to be comforted and reassured that such events will not happen to them.

The Division of Pediatricians of the Royal Australian College of Physicians is now so concerned about possible effects of television violence that they issued a report that stated that by the time most children turn eighteen, they will have spent two thousand more hours watching the television screen than they have spent in the classroom.

Television is the largest sex educator of young children today. Many learned about oral sex when watching news reports about Bill Clinton and Monica Lewinsky. To protect *your* daughter from violent, sadistic or sexually explicit material (which earns huge international royalties for film directors and producers) you should limit and supervise her television viewing. The more television sets in a house, the more watching is done. Parents should not allow their daughter to have a television set or a computer in her bedroom, as this would give her the opportunity to watch any kind of material without their knowledge.

You can, and should, complain about violent or sleazy television programs that you feel may adversely affect your children.

Call or write to the program's producer or that particular station manager, citing the program's title, viewing date and time.In addition, you should do what you can to make sure your daughter does not have access to X-rated materials. X-rated videos receive these ratings because they include sadistic violence, explicit sex, bestiality, incest and crude language. To ensure that your underage daughter is unable to rent such material (especially if she looks older than her real age), advise any video stores where your family has a membership of your daughter's birth date. Insist they enter it into their computer.

Sexually explicit and violent media may be contributing to the rate of teenage suicides, which have increased in developed countries while suicides of the elderly may have declined. The United States has a distressingly high rate of teenage suicide. Many girls who attempt or commit suicide are not dropouts but hard-working students of whom teachers and parents have high expectations. While some are depressed by problems at home or school, others are confused or alienated by the conflicting messages they receive from parents and teachers as opposed to television and other media. Advertising tells them they will be happy if they buy designer label clothes, use the right cosmetics, drink alcohol, smoke cigarettes and worship the God of Thinness.

In spite of the media, schools try hard to get the message of "safe responsible sex" across in clinical surroundings. However, the pressure to have sex that girls encounter is often *far* from clinical. In the sexually charged atmosphere of discos or parties, teenage emotions can be hard to restrain. Technicolor images of beautiful girls eagerly participating in casual unprotected sex conflict sharply with the message parents and sex educators struggle so hard to impart about sexual responsibility and how girls should value themselves. Teenage girls often feel it is "uncool" to be fearful about sex, aware that other girls of their age group are having it. A conflict of values, confusion and depression can ensue, but teenagers rarely seek advice from their parents on these occasions. Before your daughter reaches puberty, encourage her to see your general practitioner alone so she has someone older and trustworthy to whom she can confide problems of a sexual nature she may hesitate to discuss with parents.

APPENDIX

RESOURCES

Below is a list of resources from the book as well as a few others. This is by no means an exhaustive list. For more information check your local library or the Internet.

Parents Without Partners, Inc.
Main Office
1650 South Dixie Highway, Suite 510
Boca Raton, FL 33432
561-391-8833
www.parentswithoutpartners.org

The National Hope Line Network
800-SUICIDE or 800-784-2433

National Runaway Switchboard
3080 N. Lincoln Ave.
Chicago, IL 60657
800-621-4000

Parents, Family and Friends of Lesbians and Gays (PFLAG)
1726 M Street
NW Suite 400 Washington, DC 20036
(202) 467-8180
www.pflag.org

Planned Parenthood
800-230-PLAN (7526)

The National Abortion Federation
1755 Massachusetts Ave NW, Suite 600
Washington, DC 20036
800-772-9100

The National Adoption Info Clearing House
330 C Street SW
Washington, DC 20447
888-251-0075

National Eating Disorders Association
603 Stewart St
Suite 803
Seattle, Washington 98101
800-931-2237

Rape Abuse and Incest National Network
800-656-HOPE (4673)

The National Domestic Violence Hotline
800-799-SAFE (7233)

The Childhelp USA® National Child Abuse Hotline
1-800-4-A-CHILD®

ABOUT THE AUTHORS

Dr. Janet Irwin has worked in child psychiatry in Edinburgh and is now a Sexual Harassment Conciliator for the University of Queensland. She has raised two girls and when in their teens, became a sole supporting parent.

Susanna de Vries has worked in a Family Therapy Clinic and written eight books. She currently lectures part-time at the University of Queensland.